World of Reading

A Thematic Approach to Reading Comprehension 3

TEACHER'S MANUAL
with TESTS and ANSWER KEYS

Joan Baker-González
University of Puerto Rico, Mayagüez (retired)

Eileen K. Blau
University of Puerto Rico, Mayagüez

PEARSON
Longman

World of Reading 3
A Thematic Approach to Reading Comprehension
Teacher's Manual with Tests and Answer Keys

Copyright © 2009 by Pearson Education, Inc.
All rights reserved.

No part of this publication may be reproduced, stored in a retrieval system, or transmitted in any form or by any means, electronic, mechanical, photocopying, recording, or otherwise, without the prior permission of the publisher.

Pearson Education, 10 Bank Street, White Plains, NY 10606

Staff Credits: The people who made up the *World of Reading 3 Teacher's Manual with Tests and Answer Keys* team, representing editorial, production, design, and manufacturing, are Pietro Alongi, Dave Dickey, Oliva Fernandez, Ann France, Christopher Leonowicz, Martha McGaughey, Jennifer Stem, Paula Van Ells, and Pat Wosczyk.

Text composition: ElectraGraphics, Inc.
Text font: 11/13 Times

Text Credits: Page 103 "Friends as Healers" by Rebecca Stowe and Roger Rosenblatt from *Modern Maturity*, September/October 1997. **Page 108** "Do Working Moms Make Better Moms?" by Kyanna Sutton from Family Education Network, Summer 2005. **Page 113** "A Kinder, Gentler Exam Week." Reprinted with permission from *On Wisconsin Magazine*; http://life.familyeducation.com/working-parents/child-care/36134.html, University of Wisconsin Madison. **Page 117** "Punctuality: Some Cultures Are Wound Tighter Than Others" by Jane Engle. Reprinted with permission from *The Los Angeles Times*, December 11, 2005. **Page 122** "Moral Compass" by Melissa Maynard. Reprinted with permission from *Atlanta Magazine* (Vol. 47, No. 144, May 2007). **Page 127** "Environmental Tipping Points: A New Slant on Strategic Environmentalism" by Gerald Marten, Steve Brooks, and Amanda Suutari from *Worldwatch Magazine*, November/December 2005, pp. 10–14; www.worldwatch.org

ISBN-13: 978-0-13-600215-4
ISBN-10: 0-13-600215-3

PEARSON LONGMAN ON THE WEB

Pearsonlongman.com offers online resources for teachers and students. Access our Companion Websites, our online catalog, and our local offices around the world.

Visit us at **pearsonlongman.com**.

Printed in the United States of America
1 2 3 4 5 6 7 8 9 10—V0LA—13 12 11 10 09

CONTENTS

Introduction v

Chapter-by-Chapter Teaching Tips

Unit 1: Friendship
    Chapter 1 2
    Chapter 2 4
    Chapter 3 7
    Chapter 4 9

Unit 2: Parents and Children
    Chapter 5 12
    Chapter 6 16
    Chapter 7 17
    Chapter 8 18

Unit 3: Stress
    Chapter 9 21
    Chapter 10 22
    Chapter 11 25
    Chapter 12 28

Unit 4: Cultures in Contact
    Chapter 13 31
    Chapter 14 33
    Chapter 15 36
    Chapter 16 39

Unit 5: Ethics
    Chapter 17 44
    Chapter 18 46
    Chapter 19 48
    Chapter 20 53

Unit 6: The Environment
    Chapter 21 56
    Chapter 22 59
    Chapter 23 61
    Chapter 24 64

Student Book Answer Key **67**

Unit Tests
    Test Rationale 100
    Unit 1 102
    Unit 2 107
    Unit 3 112
    Unit 4 116
    Unit 5 121
    Unit 6 125

Unit Tests Answer Key **130**

Introduction

Welcome to the Teacher's Manual for *World of Reading 3*

World of Reading has been designed to enable students to read authentic materials written for adult native speakers of English. The primary difficulty students have in reading authentic material is with vocabulary. Of course, knowing the meanings of words and expressions does not guarantee better reading comprehension, as there are other important factors involved. However, the number of words needed to comprehend authentic material for adults presents a considerable hurdle.[1] Getting over this hurdle requires work and dedication on the part of students; one important role for teachers is to support their students in this undertaking. Two ways teachers can do this are to: 1. provide consistent and repeated exposure to target words and expressions students need to learn (i.e., recycle vocabulary), and 2. help students deepen their knowledge of words by learning multiple meanings for words in a variety of contexts.

Many of the tips in Part One of the *Teacher's Manual* will help you with these two tasks. First, the Recycling Vocabulary section lists vocabulary targeted in earlier readings and also provides the earlier context so you do not have to look for it. Second, exercise models give additional exposure to target words and expressions in meaningful ways. Finally, there are occasional suggestions of ways that you can help students remember the meanings of words by understanding something about their construction or etymology. In addition to helping develop students' vocabularies, the tips also provide ways to improve students' understanding of text organization and other text features.

Recall that in the Teacher's Introduction to the Student Book, you will find a full description of the series, including suggestions for how to handle different exercises. At the back of the book, there is a chapter-by-chapter list of targeted vocabulary, which should be useful in planning review activities and writing quizzes and exams. Words included in that list are targeted in one of three ways: 1. They are pre-taught at some point before reading (Unit Opener, About the Reading, Thinking about the Topic, Previewing), 2. They are included in marginal multiple-choice exercises, or 3. They are incorporated into the Vocabulary section, either in Vocabulary Building or in the second, more specialized exercise.

Part One of the *Teacher's Manual* (Chapter-by-Chapter Teaching Tips) is followed by the Student Book Answer Key, Unit Tests, and the Unit Tests Answer Key.

---

[1] It is estimated that a person needs a vocabulary of at least 3,000–5,000 word families to begin to read authentic academic materials. (Nation, Paul and Waring, Robert. [1997] "Vocabulary size, text coverage and word lists." In Schmitt, Norbert and McCarthy, Michael, eds. *Vocabulary-Description, Acquisition and Pedagogy* pp. 6–19. Cambridge University Press.) The estimate is more like 10,000 to do university work in English with reasonable ease. (Hazenberg, S. & Hulstijn, J. [1996]. "Defining a minimal receptive second-language vocabulary for non-native university students: An empirical investigation." *Applied Linguistics* 17(2), 145–163.)

Chapter-by-Chapter Teaching Tips

UNIT 1 FRIENDSHIP

Unit Opener (page 1)

As students discuss the questions and quotes, you can write words related to the unit topic on the board, either those that students use correctly in the discussion or those that they need to learn. After the discussion, have students pronounce any new words and check to see that their meaning is clear. Offer definitions and example sentences as needed. Students will probably know most vocabulary needed to discuss the questions, but you might improve the discussion by teaching students words and expressions such as: *accept a person as he/she is*, *confide in*, *respect*, and *trust*.

Do not worry if discussion of these questions is brief; students will revisit the topic of what a friend is in Thinking about the Topic for Chapter 1.

Discussing the quotes is a natural place for students to practice paraphrasing. You might want to explain what a paraphrase is at this time (*saying the same idea in different words, especially to make it clear*) and have students paraphrase the quotes here and on other Unit Opener pages. Improving students' ability to paraphrase is a focus of specific vocabulary exercises in *World of Reading 3*, beginning in Unit 2.

CHAPTER 1
All Kinds of Friends

Read (page 3)

Recycling Vocabulary

If students used *World of Reading 2*, ask them if they remember the following vocabulary items: *advice, amazed, contract, contribute to, depressed, establish, generation, horizon (on the horizon), lend, maintain, model, ongoing, promote, public, scared,* and *self-esteem*. Select words appropriate for your students, and call on volunteers to explain the meanings or provide them, if necessary. Tell students they will see these items in the reading, but perhaps with new meanings. Remind students that many words, such as *model*, can be used as different parts of speech without changing form; meanings, however, may vary.

Reading authentic writing means that students will encounter and have to deal with idiosyncrasies of individual writers. Viorst uses *ourself* (¶1) as a reflexive, rather than the usual *ourselves*, apparently to emphasize that each person is an individual self. Another way to do this would have been to use *our self*. Notice the use of *our private self* in ¶9.

You can use the sentence in line 5 of ¶3 to remind students to look for definitions in the text: "When we need <u>a lift</u>, they give us <u>a ride</u> . . ."

You can use the expression *come-and-save-me help* (¶10) to comment on the fact that English can make compound adjectives from more than the usual two words: *a black-and-blue mark; a six-and-a-half-year-old son*.

2 *World of Reading 3 Teacher's Manual*

Comprehension Check

Second Reading (page 4)

Call students' attention to the note-taking icon. Talk with them about how and when to highlight or take notes. People have different ways of marking major ideas and important details. Whatever their system, it is important for students to know that it is not useful to highlight everything.

Also, talk with students about the importance of learning to paraphrase the words of writers, that is, to express them in their own words rather than quoting. Knowing how to paraphrase is a foundation skill for summarizing without plagiarizing (*copying a writer's exact words without giving proper credit*). Learning to paraphrase is not easy. It requires knowing synonyms, synonymous expressions, and ways to vary syntax. It takes time and lots of practice to develop this ability, especially in a second language. Tell students that considerable practice is provided in this book.

Vocabulary

Vocabulary Building (page 6)

Item 5, *mentor*: The word *mentor* comes from a name. Mentor was the advisor of Telemachus, son of King Priam of Troy in Greek mythology, hence its modern meaning of "an experienced person who helps and advises a less experienced person." Other examples of words that come from proper nouns include:

sandwich: In 1762, the fourth Earl of Sandwich, John Montagu, asked for beef to be put between slices of bread so he could eat and continue gambling. Read more at: http://www.wordsources.info/words-mod-sandwich.html.

maverick (person whose behavior is surprisingly different from other people's): Samuel A. Maverick (1803–1870) was a Texas rancher who did not brand his cattle like everyone else. Read more at: http://www.thewritersplace.com/writestuff/modules.php?name=News&file=article&sid=22.

boycott: In 1880 during the Land War in Ireland, Captain Charles Boycott refused to reduce tenants' rent on land that he supervised; in fact, he evicted the tenants. In response, local people refused to deal with him. Businessmen wouldn't trade with him; the postmaster wouldn't deliver his mail. The people isolated him totally; they boycotted him. Read more at: http://www.answerbag.com/q_view/31430.

Word Analysis (page 6)

This is one of two Word Analysis exercises in *World of Reading 3* (the other is in Chapter 21). When there are not enough words to be analyzed to make an exercise, you will find analysis of some individual words in the Vocabulary Reminder List.

Vocabulary Review (page 7)

Item 4 gives you an opportunity to talk to students about collocation (*words that native speakers often put together*). Although *broaden* and *enhance* can both be used in the first blank, only *broaden* collocates with *our horizons* and, therefore, must be used in the second blank. In *World of Reading 3* students will sometimes need to use their knowledge of collocations to complete the vocabulary review correctly.

Vocabulary Reminder List

If you have not used *World of Reading 1* and *2*, in this section we remind you of things you can show students about vocabulary in the reading. They include phrasal verbs, collocations, verbs and adjectives plus the prepositions they require, synonyms and antonyms, and word analysis. Our purpose is to call things to your attention so you can decide if you want to deal with this material.

Collocations: *need a lift* (¶3), *give (someone) a ride* (¶3), *ongoing friendship* (¶9), *close friend(s)* (¶10), *take care (of)* (¶10) = help, watch out for; Viorst uses a shortened form of this collocation, but native speakers understand the ellipsis (they take care *of us*).

CHAPTER 2
Online Friendships

Read *(page 9)*

Recycling Vocabulary

If students used *World of Reading 2*, ask them if they remember the following vocabulary items: *achievement, advice, average, comment, deal, gossip, guy, keep in touch with, network, profile, tough, tremendous,* and *witness*. Select words appropriate for your students, and call on volunteers to explain the meanings or provide them, if necessary. Tell students they will see these items in the reading, but perhaps with new meanings. Remind students that many words, such as *average, comment, deal, gossip, network,* and *witness* can be used as different parts of speech without changing form; meanings, however, may vary.

The following use of *way* (¶9) is a colloquial equivalent of *much*: ". . . it would have been way harder to be away from my friends."

You may help students remember the meaning of *link* if you draw a chain on the board and label its sections *links*.

Vocabulary

Vocabulary Building *(page 13)*

Item 3, *outlet*: It might help students remember the meaning of the word *outlet* if you connect it to the expression *let out (let go of)* your emotions, anger.

Item 4, *core*: It might help students understand this use of *core* if they know that the *core* is the center of an apple.

Item 9, *bullying*: Students should understand the concept of *bullying* better if they talk about the behaviors of kids who were mean to other children during their school years.

Multiword Expressions *(page 13)*

General Information: Multiword Expressions

Multiword Expression (MWE) is a general cover term for a variety of word groups or lexical phrases where meaning is associated with a phrase, not a single word. MWEs include:

phrasal verbs	*take over* = take control of, *break up with* = end a relationship with
collocations	*spend time, a waste of time*
verb or adjective + preposition	*care about, afraid of*
idioms, proverbs, and sayings	*get out of hand, get a kick out of, Rome wasn't built in a day.*

It is important for students to learn multiword expressions as units. Learning meaningful language chunks focuses students' attention on English, instead of translating word for word from their native language. It helps them sound more like native speakers, read more efficiently, and gain fluency.

Phrasal verbs consist of two (and sometimes three) words: a verb that is followed by a particle such as *on, off, out,* or *up*. The meaning of some phrasal verbs is quite literal and easy to see; others are idiomatic, and students will need to know how to find them in their dictionaries. In Longman dictionaries, phrasal verbs follow the entry for the verb, are printed in bold face, and are followed by *phr. v.* Phrasal verbs, like other verbs, can have more than one meaning; some are slang, most are rather informal, and some can be fairly formal.

To recognize phrasal verbs when reading and to use them in writing, students need to know about the separability of these verbs.

Two-word transitive [T] phrasal verbs (*beat up, take over,* and *look over*) are generally separable. You can put a direct object (when it is a noun) either between the two parts or at the end. For example: *look* the report *over* OR *look over* the report. When the direct object is a pronoun, the verb must be separated, *look it over.* Two-word intransitive verbs [I] by definition have no object so are inseparable. For example: *sit down, stand up.* Three-word phrasal verbs such as *keep up with* and *hang out with* are inseparable; they are sometimes used intransitively without the preposition. For example, [T] I like to *hang out with* my friends. [I] It's really fun to just *hang out.*

A collocation is two or more words that native speakers use together. Learners do not necessarily recognize chunks of meaningful language when they hear or see them, so it will help if you call attention to them. To help you, phrasal verbs, collocations, and other multiword expressions that are not in specific exercises are listed in the Vocabulary Reminder List in the *Teacher's Manual*. Exercises like the one on page 6 will encourage students to pay attention to words that are used together.

(continued)

Match the words on the left with the best choice on the right to form a multiword expression. Use a match only once.

    ____ 1. IM helps teens keep ____   a. worth of junk.

    ____ 2. IM can take ____   b. in touch with friends.

    ____ 3. I just threw away a lifetime's   c. out of a dangerous situation.

    ____   d. over your life if you let it.

    ____ 4. Please look ____   e. over my composition

(Answers: 1. b, 2. d, 3. a, 4. e)

The exercise above can be given to students in abbreviated form without the context, but it is then more likely there will be more than one correct answer. For example:

    ____ 1. keep   a. worth of

    ____ 2. take   b. in touch with

    ____ 3. a lifetime's   c. out of

    ____ 4. more than you   d. over

                                                      e. like to think

Answers: (1. b, 2. c and d, 3. a, 4. e)

The more context you give, the more the focus is on total meaning rather than just recognizing the words that go together; both types of practice can be valuable.

A third, more difficult practice, can be quickly written on the board.

Fill in the blanks with a likely collocation.

1. enlarge _____ (*your community of friends, a photograph, your vocabulary*)

2. a tremendous _____ (*help, person*)

3. the bulk of their _____ (*time, money*)

4. back out _____ (*of*)

5. keep in touch with _____ (*friends, people, your parents*)

6. posing as _____ (*teenagers*)

As students increase their sensitivity to multiword expressions, ask them to identify some in the readings and suggest that they write them in their word banks and use them in their writing.

Additional Vocabulary Exercise—Nouns and Verbs With the Same Form

You might want to use this exercise to remind your students that that many English words can be both nouns and verbs (and sometimes adjectives) without adding a suffix. For a more complete presentation of the four major parts of speech, see page 10.

Circle N *if the underlined word is being used as a noun and* V *if a verb.*

1. We're going to <u>link</u> these computers in a network.   N Ⓥ
   A chain is as strong as its weakest <u>link</u>.   Ⓝ V
2. We <u>IM</u> everybody after school.   N Ⓥ
   He uses <u>IM</u> to keep in touch.   Ⓝ V

3. Don't listen to what they're saying. It's just <u>gossip</u>.   Ⓝ V
   Who <u>gossips</u> more, men or women?   N Ⓥ
4. Don't let the small things <u>upset</u> you.   N Ⓥ
   The victory was a surprising <u>upset</u>.   Ⓝ V
5. Siblings often <u>quarrel</u> to get their parents' attention.   N Ⓥ
   I had a bitter <u>quarrel</u> with a friend about money.   Ⓝ V

Ask students to write similar sentences using the following words from the reading: *place* (¶12), *level* (¶12), *offer* (¶13), *judge* (¶13), *share* (¶14), *interest* (¶14), *block* (¶17), *bully* (¶17). Remind students that recognizing the part of speech is important when they look up the word in the dictionary in order to get the correct meaning for the context. Knowing the part of speech also helps when inferring the meaning of unfamiliar vocabulary.

Vocabulary Reminder List

Phrasal verbs: *find out* [T, I] (¶2) = learn; *move back* (¶9) = return; *print off* [T] (¶16) = print quickly (parallel to *dash off* a note = write quickly); *turn in* [T] (¶16) = give to teacher/authority of some kind; *look over* = review, check (last bullet in the box)

Collocations: *go online* (¶1), *be a pretty big deal* (¶6), *a waste of time* (¶7), *leave behind* (¶9), *back home* (¶9), *avoid trouble spots* (¶19), *give (you) a real opportunity to* (¶19), *in the years ahead* (¶19)

Compound adjectives: *face-to-face* friendships (¶2), *role-playing* games (¶3), *real-world* friends (¶3), *real-life* friends (¶7); note that in ¶11, *real world* is a noun phrase, not a compound adjective.

CHAPTER 3
How Do I Like Thee? Let Me Count the Ways

Before You Read

Previewing *(page 16)*

Tell students that the words *proximity, exposure, similarity, reciprocity,* and *physical attractiveness* are in italics because they are defined in this section, making them target vocabulary words they need to learn.

Read *(page 17)*

Recycling Vocabulary

If students used *World of Reading 2*, ask them if they remember the following vocabulary items: *a good deal of, apparent, come up with, establish, evaluate, findings, initially, maintain, peer, promote,* and *questionnaire*. Select words appropriate for your students, and call on volunteers to explain the meanings or provide them, if necessary. Tell students they will see these items in the reading, but perhaps with new meanings.

The chart on page 8 lists vocabulary items from this chapter that have also appeared in earlier chapters of this book. There are several ways you can use this information. For example:

- Put the words in the left column on the board and tell students that they will see them in the new reading. Ask students if they remember the word or a related word from an earlier reading. Add the words from the right column.

Chapter-by-Chapter Teaching Tips   **7**

- For the words that vary in form, ask students what part of speech each is. For example, point out that in Chapter 1 we saw the verb *expose*. In this reading we will see the noun *exposure*.
- Ask students to provide definitions and example sentences for the words if they can. If not, provide them.

LOCATION IN CHAPTER 3	LOCATION IN EARLIER CHAPTERS
exposure (¶3)	*expose:* "although we may not expose as much . . . to each of our closest friends" (Chapter 1, ¶9)
furthermore (¶4)	*furthermore:* "Friends furthermore take care—they come if we call them at two in the morning" (Chapter 1, ¶10)

The phrase *folk wisdom* refers to the wisdom of ordinary folks or people (from German *Volk* = people); also *folk music, folklore, Volkswagen.*

Vocabulary

Vocabulary Building *(page 19)*

Item 1, *virtually*: The word *virtually* as used here tends to be more common in writing. In speaking, people often use *just about* or *almost*. Students will probably be more familiar with the term *virtual world* (referring to cyberspace) than with this use.

You may want to call students' attention to the rather formal choice of words in this selection, as would be expected in a textbook. For example: *contradicts, evoke, factors, keep confidences, peers, promotes, respondents, stemming from, traits, verdict* (primarily a legal term), *virtually* and the terms in the headings (*proximity*, etc.). You could also have students locate formal words.

Vocabulary Reminder List

Collocations: *opposites attract* (¶1)

Word Analysis: *promote* (¶4): *pro-* (before, forward) + *mot-* (from the Latin word meaning "motion, movement") = move forward, advance; Ask students if they can think of other words with "mot" in them that refer to moving (*motor, motion, motivate, demote*—an antonym for promote).

Item 3, *verdict: ver-* (Latin root meaning "true") + *dict-* (Latin root meaning "say, speak") = that which speaks the truth. Ask students if they can think of other words with "ver-", meaning "true", and "dict-", meaning "speak," in them (*verify, verification, diction, dictionary, dictate, dictator, benediction, predict*).

Item 5, *contradict: contra-* (Latin prefix meaning "against" or "contrary") + *dict-* (Latin root meaning "say, speak" = to say the opposite.) Ask students if they can think of other words with "contra-" in them (*contrast, contrary, contraceptive*). For *dict-* see Item 3 above.

Text Analysis

Academic Writing: Citing Sources *(page 20)*

Note that the Reference list showing the sources cited in this article would normally appear at the end of the article rather than on page 21 of the *Student Book*.

CHAPTER 4
The First Day of School

Read *(page 22)*

You might want to ask students if they notice something different about how lines 9–11 look on the page *(no quotation marks in the conversation or anywhere in this story)*. Some writers choose to omit them, which is another example of the idiosyncrasies found when reading authentic selections.

Recycling Vocabulary

If students used *World of Reading 2*, ask them if they remember the following vocabulary items: *amazed, ambition*. Select words appropriate for your students, and call on volunteers to explain the meanings or provide them, if necessary. Tell students they will see these items in the reading, but perhaps with new meanings.

Vocabulary

Vocabulary Building: Synonyms *(page 26)*

This is the first of several synonym exercises in the book. In addition to adding variety to their writing, knowing synonyms (and antonyms) will help students summarize and report information without plagiarizing. It is not recommended that pairs of synonyms or antonyms be presented together for the first time. However, once students know one word fairly well, they can practice them together.

It is best to think of synonyms as words with similar, not identical, meanings. There is often a difference in the level of formality (register), positive or negative associations in most people's minds (connotation), and the words they combine with (collocation). You can illustrate this with some of the words practiced in this section:

Item 1, *frightened: Frightened, afraid,* and *scared* are close synonyms. Perhaps because *frightened* and *scared* both come from transitive verbs, they clearly suggest that something put someone in this state (something *frightened* or *scared* a person). *Afraid* is related to an intransitive verb (*fear*) and seems less strong.

Item 2, *despised: Despised* and *detested* refer to a very strong disliking. *Hated* also refers to a strong disliking, but since the word *hate* is used more commonly (often overused), it doesn't seem as strong as the other two.

Item 3, *sullen: Quiet* is only a partial synonym for *sullen* because the latter suggests that a person is both quiet and somewhat angry or upset.

The remaining items show very close synonyms. Synonyms and antonyms will be called to your attention in the Vocabulary Reminder List.

Linking Readings

Once you complete Unit 1, you might want to have a class or group discussion on the following questions: 1. What similarities and differences do you see between making friends face-to-face and online? Consider the factors in Chapter 3 (proximity, etc.). 2. What are some important similarities and differences between the role of friends in the lives of children and adults?

Unit Wrap-Up

Word Families (page 28)

If students have not used *World of Reading 1* and *2*, you may need to check that they can recognize the four major parts of speech.

> **General Information: Major Parts of Speech**
>
> **Nouns** give the name of a person, place, thing, or abstract concept; they answer the questions *Who?* or *What?* Most nouns can be used with:
>
> articles (*a/an/the/some*): a box, an elephant, the newspaper, some butter
> possessives (*my, your,* etc.): my money, his children, their house
> question phrases (*How much?, How many?*): How much coffee? How many cups?
>
> **Verbs** refer to an action (*run*), mental activity (*think*), or state of being (*be, have*). In English, verbs change form when referring to now, every day, yesterday, and tomorrow (*am walking* now, *walk* every day, *walked* yesterday, *am going to walk* tomorrow). Verbs can be used after modals (*will, should, might,* etc.) and the auxiliary verbs *be* and *have* (*will* go, *should* try, *am* running, *have* seen). *To + base verb* gives the infinitive form (I like *to run*.).
>
> **Adjectives** come before nouns and follow verbs like *be, seem, look,* and *appear*. They often follow *very* and other intensifiers like *quite, really,* and *extremely*. They answer the question *What kind of?* (a *sullen* child; The child was *sullen*.)
>
> **Adverbs** of manner commonly end in *-ly*. Many adverbs are not single words, but phrases like *in the morning, at the park,* and *every day*. Adverbs and adverbial phrases answer the questions *How?* (walk *quickly*), *Where?* (walk *to the store*), *When?* (walk *in the morning*), *How often?* (walk *every day*), and *Why?* (walk *for exercise*) about the verb.

The following exercise will allow you to check that students recognize parts of speech without asking them to explain how they know.

Circle the function of the nonsense word SMOTCH for each sentence.

1. We SMOTCH every day.   N   **(V)**   Adj   Adv
2. He's a very SMOTCH teacher.   N   V   **(Adj)**   Adv
3. They want to SMOTCH the house.   N   **(V)**   Adj   Adv
4. We saw the big SMOTCH.   **(N)**   V   Adj   Adv
5. He talks very SMOTCHLY.   N   V   Adj   **(Adv)**
6. I can't SMOTCH with you today.   N   **(V)**   Adj   Adv
7. They seem very SMOTCH.   N   V   **(Adj)**   Adv
8. Do you have any SMOTCHES?   **(N)**   V   Adj   Adv

After students have studied the Word Families chart and done the exercise, ask them to find suffixes that mark each of the four parts of speech:

Nouns: *-ology, -tion/-ition/-sion, -ure, -ial, -ness,* and *-ity*

Verbs: *-ize, ify*

Adjectives: *-etic, -ous, -ory, -ive*

Adverbs: *-ly*

Ask students for examples of other words that use these suffixes. Beware that a few adjectives end in *-ly* (*friendly, lovely*).

Shifting Primary Stress

Correct location of the primary stress on a word is critically important to a native speaker's understanding of the word. For example, if the word *control* is pronounced CONtrol, rather than conTROL, it is likely a native speaker will have trouble understanding. The following words in the Word Families in Unit 1 show a shift in primary stress:

aPOLogy, aPOLogize	apoloGETic (-ally)
expoSItion	exPOsure, exPOSE, exPOSitory
obliGAtion	OBligate, oBLIGatory (-ily)

Go over the chart on page 28 of the *Student Book* with students, checking their pronunciation of the words. The exercise in the Word Families section of the Unit Wrap-Up uses only a few of the words that are listed in the chart. Time permitting, maximize use of the information in the chart by having students use other words from the unit in oral or written sentences.

You may want to show the word families for two other words in this unit, *deny* and *frank*, and have students choose the word that correctly completes the sentence.

A.	denial	deny		
B.	frankness		frank	frankly

1. Many people ___deny___ problems that are obvious to their friends and families, such as problems with alcohol. They are in ___denial___ about these problems.
2. I'm a very direct person. ___Frankly___, I think you are making a mistake.

Polysemous Words (page 29)

To help students learn multiple meanings of these words, have them make word bank cards that illustrate at least two meanings of the word in the correct context. For example, write on the board:

    maintain: 1. support financially _____

                 2. keep in good condition _____

Students can use sentences from the reading, example sentences from the *Longman Advanced American Dictionary*, or original sentences if you have time to check the accuracy of the students' work. If students write original sentences, show them how to give enough context in their sentences to demonstrate that they know the meanings of the word. For example:

- *We have to maintain the house.* (unacceptable; The sentence does not show what *maintain* means. It could just as well mean *sell* as *keep in good condition*.)

- *It's important to maintain property. You should check and repair problems regularly so the property doesn't lose value.* (acceptable; The sentences give enough context to show that *maintain* means keep something in good condition.)

Recommended Readings and Websites

Fulghum, Robert. "The Barber." In *All I Need to Know I Learned in Kindergarten*. New York: Villard Books, a division of Random House, Inc., 1986.

    The author's observations and thoughts about another category of friend.

Brooks, Martha. "A Boy and His Dog." In *Who Do You Think You Are? Stories of Friends and Enemies*. Edited by Hazel Rochman and Darlene Z. McCampbell. New York and Boston: Little, Brown, and Co. (Hachette Group), 1993.

> The story of a young teenage boy who received his dog as a present on his first birthday and now must deal with the dog's terminal illness.

Reynolds, Quentin. "A Secret for Two." Alger, Andrew, and Rohlfs, 1936.

> This story about a friendship between a man and his horse is in *World of Reading 1*, Chapter 8. For students who didn't use that book, it can be found online through The Literature Network at http://www.online-literature.com.

Peck, Richard. "Priscilla and the Wimps." In *Who Do You Think You Are? Stories of Friends and Enemies*. Edited by Hazel Rochman and Darlene Z. McCampbell. New York and Boston: Little, Brown and Co. (Hachette Group), 1993.

> A story about an unlikely pair of friends and how they handle the bullying of gang members in their school.

Students can read other people's stories of friendship and submit their own at http://www.best-friends-forever.com/friendship-stories.html.

UNIT 2: PARENTS AND CHILDREN

Unit Opener (page 31)

As students discuss the questions and quotes, you can write words related to the unit topic on the board, either those that students use correctly in the discussion or those that they need to learn. After the discussion, have students pronounce any new words and check to see that their meaning is clear. Offer definitions and example sentences as needed. Students will probably know most vocabulary needed to discuss the questions, but you might improve the discussion by teaching students words and expressions such as *single parent, nuclear family, extended family,* and *role model.*

CHAPTER 5
Mother Was Really Somebody

Before You Read

Thinking about the Topic (page 32)

This is the first of several extended Thinking about the Topic sections in this book. They provide background information which should deepen students' understanding of the unit topic and the topic of this reading. Hopefully, this information will lead to more interesting discussions.

Read *(page 33)*

Recycling Vocabulary

If students used *World of Reading 2*, ask them if they remember the following vocabulary items: *accomplish/accomplishment, achievement, anxious, certificate/certified as, comment (on), crowd, devoted to, environment, eventually, on the horizon, influence, make up for, manage to, potential, pray, quit, raise (kids), reflect on, security, self-esteem, shiver, thriving/thrive, trade,* and *urban*. Select words appropriate for your students, and call on volunteers to explain the meanings or provide them, if necessary. Tell students they will see these items in the reading, but perhaps with new meanings.

Refer to pages 7–8 for ideas on how to review these words in meaningful activities.

LOCATION IN CHAPTER 5	LOCATION IN EARLIER CHAPTERS
confidence (¶12, 15)	*confidences*: "people identified the qualities most valued in a friend as the ability to keep confidences" (Chapter 3, ¶6)
delighted (¶8)	*delighted*: "The housekeeper was delighted." (Chapter 4, line 131)
mentor (¶3)	*mentor*: "Each role, as mentor or quester, . . . offers gratifications of its own." (Chapter 1, ¶8)

Students may remember what *puzzled* (MMC) means if they know that a puzzle is a game or toy with a lot of pieces to fit together. Puzzles, especially with lots of pieces of the same color, can be confusing.

A *jolt* (MMC) is a sudden strong movement; a person can wake up *with a jolt*, stop *with a jolt*, or receive a terrible *jolt* in a car accident.

Strong is a partial meaning of *indomitable* (MMC). You might want to connect it to the word *dominate* (have power over) and *dominant* gene (a stronger gene). An *indomitable spirit* cannot be defeated; nothing can overpower it.

You might want to use the collocation, *unstinting praise* (¶17), to remind students of the second step in dealing with unfamiliar vocabulary mentioned in the Student's Introductory Chapter (page xviii)—recognizing that some words are nonessential and can be skipped, at least on the first reading. When reading authentic readings, students will probably find quite a few words they do not know. They should interrupt their reading to look up words in a dictionary only when they cannot understand what seem to them to be important ideas.

Vocabulary

Vocabulary Building *(page 37)*

Item 1, *manage to*: You can use this expression to remind students how important small words can be. If they do not pay attention to the preposition *to*, they will misunderstand the writer. The sentence is not about how the Michelottis managed their children in top colleges.

Using a Dictionary *(page 38)*

Additional Exercise: Reviewing Dictionary Use

Before doing the *Student Book* exercise on page 38, you might want to review dictionary skills using the questions on page 15 and the entries for *burst* from the *Longman Advanced American Dictionary*. Students encounter *burst* in ¶35 on page 36 of the *Student Book*.

First remind students of the steps required to use the dictionary correctly:

1. Read the sentence carefully to determine the part of speech of the word.
2. Find the entry for the appropriate part of speech in the dictionary.
3. Read the individual definitions and examples to find the one that makes sense in the context.
4. Look for phrasal verbs and other expressions in boldface after the entries for the main word.

burst¹ /bəːst/ *v. past tense and past participle* **burst**
1 BREAK OPEN [I,T] if something bursts, or if you burst it, it breaks apart suddenly and violently because of the pressure on it, so that the substance it contains comes out: *The kids were trying to burst the balloons by sitting on them. / A bag of flour had burst open in the cupboard. / After days of heavy rain, the dam finally burst.* ➤ see THESAURUS box at **break¹**
2 be bursting with sth INFORMAL to be filled with something, or have a lot of something: *The window boxes were bursting with flowers. / a story bursting with ideas* / **be bursting with pride/confidence/energy etc.** *Her parents watched, bursting with pride, as she walked on stage.* ➤ see also **be bursting at the seams** at SEAM (4)
3 MOVE SUDDENLY [I always + adv./prep.] to move somewhere suddenly or quickly, especially in or out of a place: **+ through/into/in etc.** *Four men burst into the store and tied up the clerks. / The door **burst open** (= suddenly opened) and the kids piled into the house.*
4 RIVER **burst its banks** if a river bursts its banks, water comes over the top of the river banks and goes onto the land around it
5 burst the/sb's bubble to make someone suddenly realize that something is not as good as they believed or hoped: *I hate to burst your bubble, but you look really dumb in that hat.*
6 burst a blood vessel SPOKEN to become extremely angry
7 be bursting to do sth INFORMAL to want to do something very much
[Origin: Old English *berstan*] ➤ see also OUTBURST

burst in on/upon sb/sth *phr. v.* to enter a room suddenly and interrupt something, in a way that embarrasses you or other people: *I burst in on them, thinking that the room was empty.*

burst into sth *phr. v.* **1** to suddenly begin to make a sound, especially to start singing, crying, or laughing: *The audience burst into wild applause. / As he worked, he would often **burst into song**. Ken's sister suddenly burst into tears while we were eating.* **2 burst into flames** to suddenly start to burn: *The aircraft burst into flames.*

burst out *phr. v.* **1 burst out laughing/crying etc.** to suddenly start to laugh, cry, etc.: *Rubin burst out laughing as he read the letter.* **2** to suddenly say something in a forceful way: *"I don't believe you!" she burst out angrily.*

burst² /n. [C] **1** a short sudden increase in effort or activity: *I try to work **in short bursts**. / + of The industry has seen a burst of activity recently. /* **a burst of speed/energy** *a burst of speed at the finish line* **2 a burst of sth a)** a short sudden and usually low sound: *a burst of machine-gun fire* **b)** a sudden strong feeling or emotion: *a burst of anger* **3** the act of something bursting or the place where it has burst: *a burst in the pipe*

14 *World of Reading 3 Teacher's Manual*

> How does the dictionary mark separate meanings? (*boldfaced numbers*)
>
> What do the words in small capital letters show? (*the different meanings of the word—that the word is polysemous*)
>
> How are example sentences marked? (*italics*)
>
> Where can you find the pronunciation for words? (*between slash bars / /*)
>
> What parts of speech can the word *burst* be? (*both v. and n.—note there are two entries, burst¹ and burst²*)
>
> What are the past tense and the past participle of the verb *burst*? (*burst*)
>
> What phrasal verbs does *burst* participate in? What do they mean? (*burst in on/upon, burst into, burst out*)
>
> Paraphrase the following sentences using *burst*.
>
> 1. Mr. and Mrs. Michelotti were bursting with pride at Joseph's graduation from medical school. (*were filled with pride*)
> 2. I got a second burst of energy halfway through the race. (*short, sudden increase*)
> 3. When we entered the room, the people burst into applause. (*started suddenly clapping*)
> 4. The water main burst. (*broke open*)
> 5. I think the news will burst his bubble. (*make him realize he's not so great*)

Vocabulary Reminder List

Phrasal verbs: *put on* [T] (¶21) = produce; *show up* [I] (¶22) = be present, come, go; *reflect on* [T-not separable] (¶24) = influence opinion about; *call out* [T, I] (¶26) = say loudly; *get up* [I] (¶30, 32) = get out of bed

Collocations: *look like* (¶6) = appear as; *hit-and-run accident* (¶7), *quit (her) job* (¶8), *reach (our) potential* (¶8), *bolster (our) confidence* (¶12), *wouldn't hear of it* (¶13), *do anything you put your mind to* (¶16), *blueprint for success* (¶17), *current events* (¶17), *do (something) the best you can* (¶26), *I just wanted to make sure you were okay.* (¶32), *bursting with pride* (¶35)

Verb + preposition: *reach for* (¶1), *reach toward* (¶6), *trade (something) for (something)* (¶8), *apply for* (¶19), *earn (money) for* (¶19), *write/tell about* (¶20)

Compound adjectives: *medical-school* dean (¶1), *high-school* class (¶5) / *high-school* junior (¶21), *self-taught* (¶7), *paint-by-number* pictures (¶13), *41-story* building (¶14), *one-room* schoolhouse (¶17), *sleepy-eyed* (¶32)

You might want to remind students that the noun following a number in a compound adjective (five-*minute* walk) is not plural, nor do other adjectives have plural forms in English. This is a common problem for some students who confuse *I have a six-year-old son* and *My son is six years old.*

CHAPTER 6
The Problems of Fathers and Sons

Before You Read

Thinking about the Topic *(page 40)*

In general, we prefer not to pre-teach vocabulary, especially at this level, because dealing with unfamiliar vocabulary effectively while reading is a skill students must develop to read authentic material. However, this reading is an exception because without knowledge of the words showing negative feelings, students will not understand it. As you will note, we give both the noun and adjective forms of the words but give examples only for the adjectives because they are more useful to students than the noun forms.

Guilt and *shame* are very close in meaning and are used to define each other. However, they are used in different situations and expressions. *Guilty* is used in courts (a *verdict of guilty or not guilty*) while *shame* appears in the expressions *Shame on you, You should be ashamed,* and *There's nothing to be ashamed of. Ashamed* is often defined as "embarrassed," but *guilty* is not.

Read *(page 41)*

Recycling Vocabulary

If students used *World of Reading 2*, ask them if they remember the following vocabulary items: *accurately, articulate, complex, determine/determination, disappointment, dissatisfied, embarrassing, eventually, fascinating, humiliation, ignore/ignorance, nervous/nervously, quit, scream, single,* and *weep/wept*. Select words appropriate for your students, and call on volunteers to explain the meanings or provide them, if necessary. Tell students they will see these items in the reading, but perhaps with new meanings.

Refer to pages 7–8 for ideas on how to review these words in meaningful activities.

LOCATION IN CHAPTER 6	LOCATION IN EARLIER CHAPTERS
exhaustion (¶14)	*exhausted:* "Confused and exhausted, I (Joseph Michelotti) called home in tears." (Chapter 5, ¶31)
stumble (¶14)	*stumbling:* "Stumbling into the elevator, I wondered who had come to see me at that hour." (Chapter 5, ¶32)

A *Social Security card* (¶9), showing a person's name and 9-digit number, is needed to work in the United States and serves as a national identification card. Babies born in the United States now receive their Social Security number at birth.

Comprehension Check

Second Reading *(page 44)*

Remind students that if there is no evidence in the text, the statement will be an unreasonable inference. Coming to a conclusion with absolutely no evidence is often called "jumping to a conclusion."

Vocabulary

Vocabulary Building: Using Paraphrases *(page 44)*

If students ask native speakers who are not teachers for help with understanding a reading, they are likely to get a response such as, "What the writer is saying is that . . ." in which the focus is on the meaning of the whole, not on individual words. This type of exercise will help students understand this type of explanation. Hopefully, exposing them to paraphrasing will help them acquire this ability, an academic skill needed for summarizing. After students have used the paraphrase to understand as many of the difficult words as possible, you can tell them to use their dictionaries to confirm their understanding and get more information, such as example sentences.

Using a Dictionary: Words that Paint Pictures *(page 46)*

Before directing students to use their dictionaries, have them check the context in the indicated paragraph (found in column 1) and tell you what words help them understand the general, or partial meaning (in column 2). Then they can use their dictionaries to fill in column 3.

Vocabulary Reminder List

Phrasal verbs: *look on* [I] (¶11) = watch

Collocations: *I find/found it hard to accept that* (¶2), *beyond (his) grasp*

Compound Adjectives: *tight-lipped* determination (¶9), *hyphen-like* lines (¶9), *ever-so-slow* copying (¶11), *guilt-ridden* (¶15)

Word analysis: *overlapping* (¶9); Remind students that knowing one part of a word and paying attention to the context (*overlapping letters*) can help them remember the meaning of the whole word; the prefix *over-* means "on top of," so *overlap* means "one letter on top of another." Note also that this word is one that can be easily illustrated.

CHAPTER 7
Greener Grass

Read *(page 48)*

Recycling Vocabulary

If students used *World of Reading 2*, ask them if they remember the following vocabulary items: *public, security*. Select words appropriate for your students and call on volunteers to explain the meanings or provide them, if necessary. Tell students they will see these items in the reading, but they might have new meanings.

Refer to pages 7–8 for ideas on how to review these words in meaningful activities.

LOCATION IN CHAPTER 7	LOCATION IN EARLIER CHAPTER
show up (¶5)	*showed up*: "The whole family showed up." (Chapter 5, ¶22)

After reading and discussing this selection, you may want to ask students why the author chose the title "Greener Grass" to see if they understand the double entendre in the title. The title can tie José's situation to the proverb in gloss 1 (*José came to the United States because the grass looked greener there, but he found definite negatives in the United States.*). In addition, there is the connection to his occupation as a landscaper.

Vocabulary

Vocabulary Building (*page 51*)

Item 5 and Item 7, *nod, shrug*: These words are a reminder to demonstrate or have students demonstrate the meaning of words, when possible.

Vocabulary Reminder List

Phrasal verbs: *go back* [I] (¶8) = return

Collocations: *take care of* (¶1) = be responsible for, maintain; *in business for (her)self* (¶1), *left behind* (¶8)

Chapter 8
Love, Your Only Mother

Read (*page 53*)

Recycling Vocabulary

If students used *World of Reading 2*, ask them if they remember the following vocabulary items: *deposit, safe deposit box,* and *pursue*. Select words appropriate for your students, and call on volunteers to explain the meanings or provide them, if necessary. Tell students they will see these items in the reading, but perhaps with new meanings.

Refer to pages 7–8 for ideas on how to review these words in meaningful activities.

LOCATION IN CHAPTER 8	LOCATION IN EARLIER CHAPTERS
frightened (¶20)	*frightened:* "The housekeeper knew how frightened a little boy could be about going to school." (Chapter 4, line 25)
nod (¶13)	*nodding:* "Yes," he said, nodding slowly." (Chapter 7, ¶8)
point out (¶13)	*pointing out:* "She even served as tour guide, pointing out landmarks" (Chapter 5, ¶18)
rage (¶15)	*rage:* "I'll admit being mad but not blind with rage." (Chapter 1, ¶4)

Note that the writer of this story, like William Saroyan ("First Day of School," Chapter 4), does not use quotation marks to mark direct speech.

Vocabulary

Vocabulary Reminder List

Phrasal verbs: *pull out* [T] (¶12) = get from a storage place like a shelf; *look up* [T] (¶12, 15) = find in a reference book; *point out* [T] (¶13) = show, especially when using a finger to point; *come back* [I] (¶14, 19, 20) = return

Collocations: *I vowed I'd never . . .* (¶7)

Synonyms: *mull over* (MMC) (¶8) / *ponder* (¶15)

Linking Readings

Once you complete Unit 2, you might want to have a class or group discussion on the following questions: 1. Under what circumstances do families in these readings get divided? What are other circumstances leading to separation of families? How are children affected and what can be done to minimize the negative effects on children? 2. How common is it for children to have negative feelings about their parents? What causes such negative feelings and how serious are they? (Note that in Unit 1, Chapter 1, Viorst says that close friends can be closer than family and that advice from an older cross-generational friend is sometimes more likely to be accepted "as wise, not intrusive.")

Unit Wrap-Up

Word Families *(page 58)*

The following words in the Word Families in Unit 2 show a shift in primary stress. Draw students' attention to them.

    consoLAtion   conSOLE, inconSOLable (-ally)

    frusTRAtion   FRUStrate, FRUStrated, FRUStrating

Note that the word *ashamed* (item 9) is used to describe how people feel when they do something bad; *shameful* behavior is so bad that a person should feel *ashamed*.

For an explanation of when to use the participial adjectives (-ed, -ing), see page 69 in the *Student Book*.

Recommended Readings

Lazarus, Mel. "Angry Fathers." *The New Times Magazine*, May 28, 1995: 216–7.

(and)

Richman, Irwin. *Borscht Belt Bungalows: Memories of Catskill Summers*. Philadelphia: Temple University Press, 2003.

    A father teaches his 9-year old son a lesson about an unusual way to discipline a child who has participated in vandalism.

Greene, Bette. "Ordinary Woman." In *Sixteen Short Stories by Outstanding Writers for Young Adults*. Edited by Donald R. Gallo. New York: Bantam Doubleday Dell Books for Young Readers, 1984.

    A mother realizes that the only way to deal with her daughter's addiction is through tough love.

Carver, Raymond. "Little Things." (originally "Popular Mechanics") In *Where I'm Calling From: Selected Short Stories*. New York: Atlantic Monthly Press, 1991.

(and in)

Shapard, Robert and Thomas, James. Sudden Fiction: *American Short-Short Stories*. Layton, Utah: Gibbs M. Smith, Inc, 1986.

A story about a young couple fighting over their baby in the midst of a separation.

Hayden, Robert. "Those Winter Sundays." In *Angle of Ascent, New and Selected Poems*. New York: Liveright Publishing, 1975.

Poem about the thoughts of an adult son looking back on the things his father did for him as a child.

Pastan, Linda. "To a Daughter Leaving Home." In *The Imperfect Paradise*. New York: W. W. Norton, 1988. Also in *World of Reading 2*, Chapter 4.

Poem in which teaching a child to ride a bicycle is a metaphor for the child's becoming independent.

UNIT 3 STRESS

Unit Opener (page 62)

As students discuss the questions and quotes, you can write words related to the unit topic on the board, either those that students use correctly in the discussion or those that they need to learn. After the discussion, have students pronounce any new words and check to see that their meaning is clear. Offer definitions and example sentences as needed. Students will probably know most vocabulary needed to discuss the questions, but you might improve the discussion by teaching students words and expressions such as: *pressure, cope with*, and *release*.

Note also that useful vocabulary is included in the first quote. It may be necessary to help students see the humor in the second quote. Ask them if they know people who are so out-of-touch with reality, that they aren't stressed about anything, and that maybe "ignorance is bliss." (To appreciate the humor you have to agree with Tomlin that reality is stressful.)

CHAPTER 9
Plain Talk about Handling Stress

Read *(page 64)*

Recycling Vocabulary

If students used *World of Reading 2*, ask them if they remember the following vocabulary items: *actually, advice, at once, bored, come up with, deal with, expert, focus, get stuck, initial, lack, major, nervous, pressure, professional, release, resist, resource, satisfaction, seek, tune out,* and *unique*. Select words appropriate for your students, and call on volunteers to explain the meanings or provide them, if necessary. Tell students they will see these items in the reading, but they might have new meanings.

Refer to pages 7–8 for ideas on how to review these words in meaningful activities.

LOCATION IN CHAPTER 9	LOCATION IN EARLIER CHAPTERS
accomplish (¶14)	*accomplished:* "Your father has accomplished so much . . ." (Chapter 5, ¶10) *accomplishments:* praising even our most ordinary accomplishments (Chapter 5, ¶12)
commuter, commuting (¶5)	*commuted:* "He (Mr. Michelotti) worked the land and commuted to the city to run his business." (Chapter 5, ¶8)
exhaustion (¶5)	*exhausted:* "Confused and exhausted, I (Joseph Michelotti) called home in tears." (Chapter 5, ¶31) *exhaustion:* "I finally flung myself on the recently watered lawn and wept into a state of complete exhaustion." (Chapter 6, ¶14)
frowns (¶8)	*frowning:* "Ohio?" he (José) said, frowning. "That is near Memphis?" (Chapter 7, ¶10)
frustrating (¶3), *frustration* (¶5), *frustrated* (¶13)	*frustration:* "Once, during a period of deepening frustration, I told my mother that we ought to teach him how to read and write." (Chapter 6, ¶7)
sense of (¶17)	*sense of:* "followed closely by supportiveness, frankness, and a sense of humor" (Chapter 3, ¶6)

Vocabulary

Vocabulary Building *(page 67)*

Item 1, *crises:* The pronunciation of the singular and plural of this word is difficult for many students, *crisis* (like SISter) and *crises* (like SEES). This irregular plural form tends to appear with words of Greek origin (*basis/bases, diagnosis/diagnoses*).

Item 2, *overwhelmed:* Remind students that knowing one part of a word and paying attention to the context can help them remember the meaning of the whole word; the prefix *over-* means "too much, too many, too great a degree." Ask students to provide other words that use this prefix with the same meaning (*overcharge, overcook, overdose, overdue, overheat, overpay, overpopulated, overqualified, oversimplify, overweight*).

Vocabulary Reminder List

Phrasal verbs: *pull out* [I] (¶5) = drive from one lane or road into another; *tighten up* [I] (¶5); *deal with* [T-not separable] (¶7, 11) = handle; *come up with* [T] (¶7) = produce; *check (them) off* [T] (¶14) = put a check mark on a list; *take away* [T] (¶18) = remove

In ¶5, students may notice that *tighten* and *tighten up* appear with essentially the same meaning. The particle *up* may be seen to intensify the meaning of the verb or add a sense of completeness (also *burn* and *burn up, eat* and *eat up*).

Collocations: *ease tension* (¶7), *take care of* (¶11, 14) = pay attention to, care for; *release tension* (¶16), *see (something) in a different light* (¶9), *seek professional help* (¶9), *avoid problems* (¶9), *beyond (your) control* (¶10), *keep you from doing something* (¶11), *need a break from* (¶12), *prescription medications / over-the-counter medications* (¶18)

CHAPTER 10
Energy Walks

Before You Read

Previewing *(page 71)*

Remind students that italicized words are targets and are listed in the Vocabulary List at the back of their book.

Read *(page 71)*

Recycling Vocabulary

If students used *World of Reading 2*, ask them if they remember the following vocabulary items: *actually, advice, average, cut down, expect, findings, impressive/impressed, invest, marital, mood, optimism, pressure, quit, rate,* and *shift*. Select words appropriate for your students, and call on volunteers to explain the meanings or provide them, if necessary. Tell students they will see these items in the reading, but perhaps with new meanings.

Refer to pages 7–8 for ideas on how to review these words in meaningful activities.

LOCATION IN CHAPTER 10	LOCATION IN EARLIER CHAPTERS
apparent (¶3)	*apparent:* "This finding, which contradicts the values that most people say they hold, is apparent even in childhood."(Chapter 3, ¶5)
attractive (¶5)	*attract:* "knowledge about the factors that initially attract two people" (Chapter 3, ¶1) *attraction:* "increases the likelihood of interpersonal attraction." (Chapter 3, ¶4) *attractiveness:* "Physical attractiveness." (Chapter 3, ¶5)
boring (¶1)	*bored:* "One way to keep from getting bored" (Chapter 9, ¶13)
burst (¶9) (n.)	*bursting:* "And she (Mrs. Michelotti) would be bursting with pride." (Chapter 5, ¶35)
enhanced (¶9)	*enhance:* "They (friends) enhance our self-esteem" (Chapter 1, ¶1)
eventually (¶9)	*eventually:* "Yet he (Mr. Michelotti) eventually built a small, successful wholesale candy business." (Chapter 5, ¶7) "Eventually, he (Mr. López) did learn to write two words—his name and surname." (Chapter 6, ¶9)
fast-paced (¶2)	*pace:* "Unfortunately, many people try to relax at the same pace that they lead the rest of their lives." (Chapter 9, ¶19)
reaction (¶9)	*reaction:* "his initial alarm reaction may include fear of an accident" (Chapter 9, ¶5)
show up (¶8)	*show up:* "José and his sons didn't show up for two weeks." (Chapter 7, ¶5)
similar (¶8)	*similar:* "We tend to like those who are similar to us." (Chapter 3, ¶4) *similarity:* "One reason similarity increases the likelihood of interpersonal attraction" (Chapter 3, ¶4)
tension (¶3–9, 12)	*tension:* "Take some deep breaths; they also release tension." (Chapter 9, ¶16)

Vocabulary

Vocabulary Building *(page 74)*

Item 1, *lecture:* The origin of this word is the Latin word for "reading," so this word is a false cognate for speakers of Spanish and other Romance languages. The word took on its meaning of a discourse for purposes of instruction in the mid-16th century. It began to appear as a verb by the end of the century. You might use this information to interest students in how the meanings of words change.

Item 6, *ensure/insure:* Students may ask about the difference between these words. According to page 836 of the *Longman Advanced American Dictionary*, *ensure* is a more formal version of *insure*; but only *insure* is used as the verb related to *insurance*.

Item 8, *sedative:* The earliest use of this word in English dates from the early 15th century. Its usage as a noun referring to a drug dates from the late 18th century. According to etymologyonline.com, the verb *sedate* (to give sedatives) appeared in 1945. This word gives you an opportunity to show students how some new words come into a language by removing what appears to be a suffix (back formation).

Vocabulary Reminder List

Phrasal verbs: *coming up* [I] (¶2) = in the near future; *show up* [I] (¶8) = appear; *cut down* [I] (¶12) = reduce; *light up* [I] (¶12) = light a cigarette (informal)

Collocations: *reduce tension* (¶3), *make it clear that* (¶5), *a burst of energy* (¶9), *a (stubborn) weight problem* (¶10), *at fixed times* (¶10), *invest a lot of time and money* (¶13)

Synonyms: *enhanced* (¶9) = increased (¶7,8); used to modify *energy* in this article. The alternation of these synonyms gives you an opportunity to point out that writers use synonyms so they don't have to repeat the same word all the time.

Modifiers of Nouns: The reading in this chapter lends itself well to a review of different structures that modify nouns. Ask students to find examples of the following kinds of modifiers:

Participial Adjectives (-ing/-ed): *boring* (¶1), *fast-paced* (¶2), *exhausting* (¶2), *fattening* (¶3), *middle-aged* (¶4), *tired* (¶5, 9), *energizing* (¶5), *energized* (¶6), *increased* (¶7, 8, 11), *average-sized* (¶8), *enhanced* (¶9), *fixed* (¶10), *nonwalking* (¶12), *relaxed* (¶13)

Compound Adjectives: *10-minute* walk (¶2, 4, 10), *fast-paced* (¶2), *middle-aged* people (¶4), *bare-walled* room (¶5), *three-mile* walk (¶5), *three-week* period (¶6), *average-sized* candy bar (¶8), *five-minute* walks (¶12), *free-smoking* periods (¶12); You might want to remind students that the noun following a number in a compound adjective (five-*minute* walk) is not plural, nor do other adjectives have plural forms in English.

Noun Modifiers (nouns used as if they were adjectives): *energy walk* (title), *candy bar* (subhead), *candy machine* (¶1), *lecture hall* (¶1), *test anxiety* (¶2), *mood changes* (¶3), *mood shift* (¶5), *blood pressure* (¶5), *sugar snack* (¶8), *energy boost* (¶9), *sugar sedative* (¶11)

Adjective strings: *long and boring* lecture (¶1), *short, rapid* walks (¶3), *chronic personal* problems (¶11), *interesting psychological* effects (¶12)

Text Analysis

Text Organization *(page 76)*

Additional Questions

Ask students if they can find a statement of the main idea of this article reporting research. They probably will not be able to do so because it takes all of ¶3 to summarize the research, which the writer then explains in detail in the remainder of the article. The organization seen in this article is typical of writing which reports research in that it gives an overview of the research (a summary) first and then discusses methods used and the detailed results.

Responding to Reading (page 76)

If your students are going to run the survey (item 3), have them make a simple report form to use with each person they talk to. For example:

Gender: M   F
Age: _____ under 30   _____ 30–60   _____ over 60
Suffer from stress: Y   N
Causes: _____
How do you relieve stress? _____
Exercise: Y   N   Type: _____
How does it make you feel? _____

CHAPTER 11
Part 1: Stressed to Death / Part 2: Heartfelt Fear

Read (page 77)
Recycling Vocabulary

If students used *World of Reading 2*, ask them if they remember the following vocabulary items: (Part 1) *actually, argue, complex, finding, maintain, perceive, portion, pressure, primary, questionnaire,* and *recruit*; (Part 2) *actually, capacity, finding, impaired, incident, initial, pressure, recover, regulation, release, terrible,* and *trigger*. Select words appropriate for your students, and call on volunteers to explain the meanings or provide them, if necessary. Tell students they will see these items in the reading, but perhaps with new meanings.

Refer to pages 7–8 for ideas on how to review these words in meaningful activities.

Part 1:

LOCATION IN CHAPTER 11	LOCATION IN EARLIER CHAPTERS
assessed (¶6)	*assess:* "one group of people repeatedly assessed the severity of a continuing personal problem" (Chapter 10, ¶10)
chronically (¶4)	*chronic:* "After the walk, chronic personal problems appeared less serious." (Chapter 10, ¶11)
exciting (¶9)	*excited:* "it can be easy to get excited and 'sound too mean' about somebody in an IM." (Chapter 2, ¶11) *unexciting:* "Without stress, life would be dull and unexciting." (Chapter 9, ¶1)
pacemaker (¶9)	*pace:* "Unfortunately, many people try to relax at the same pace that they lead the rest of their lives." (Chapter 9, ¶19) *fast-paced:* "moderately fast-paced but not exhausting" (Chapter 10, ¶2)
prolonged (¶1)	*prolonged:* "When stress becomes prolonged . . . , it can become harmful" (Chapter 9, ¶4)
sense of (¶9)	*sense of:* "a sense of humor" (Chapter 3, ¶6) "a sense of peace and tranquility." (Chapter 9, ¶17)
strain (¶8)	*strain:* "A little give and take . . . will reduce the strain" (Chapter 9, ¶15)
tension (subhead)	*tense:* "This might explain why people who ate candy bars subsequently felt tense." (Chapter 10, ¶9) *tension:* "rate their feelings of energy and tension using a short checklist." (Chapter 10, ¶4)
tips (¶2)	*tip:* "he thanked me for the tip." (Chapter 10, ¶1)

Part 2:

LOCATION IN CHAPTER 11	LOCATION IN EARLIER CHAPTERS
link (v.) (subhead)	linked: "teens spend a lot of time linked in cyberspace." (Chapter 2, ¶1)
points out (¶8)	pointing out: "She (Mrs. Michelotti) even served as tour guide, pointing out landmarks." (Chapter 5, ¶18) point out: "I'd point out where you were in the atlas" (Chapter 8, ¶13)
showed up (¶2)	show up: "José and his sons didn't show up for two weeks." (Chapter 7, ¶5) "But one hour after snacking, some negative changes began to show up" (Chapter 10, ¶8)

Part 1:

Three of the MMC's illustrate that a person can infer a general meaning for the word or expression but will need a dictionary to understand the specific meaning.

The phrase *whittled down to nubs* means that something is gradually made smaller by taking parts away until only small rounded pieces are left.

The word *underpinnings* refers to having support from underneath.

The word *striking* has the additional meaning of *impressive*.

Students may benefit from connecting the adjective *upcoming* to the phrasal verb *come up*. Example: We have two concerts *coming up* in the next month.

Part 2:

Students may benefit from knowing that *trigger* as a noun is the part of a gun you pull to shoot it, causing the bullet to leave the gun.

The instructions in the *Student Book* ask students to preview both readings and choose one. If your class uses this option, you may want to have students do the Comprehension Checks with a classmate who read the same part and then share what they learned with classmates who read the other part. You can also have students read one part in class and the other for homework, or have students read both parts and discuss them as a class.

If all students do not read the article "Stressed to Death," (Chapter 11, Part 1), you will need to modify the unit test to eliminate *immune* from the cloze exercise and *plays a role* from the matching.

Vocabulary

Vocabulary Reminder List

Part 1:

Phrasal verbs: *chew off* [T] (¶2) = remove; *stressed out* (¶10) = adjective based on the phrasal verb *stress (somebody) out*

Collocations: *look like* (¶5) = appear, seem to be; *further tests showed* (¶8), *stressed to death* (title), *provocative findings* (the findings . . . are very provocative) (¶9), *in the best sense of the word* (¶9)

Part 2:

Phrasal verbs: *bring on* [T,I] (¶1, 8) = cause; *show up* [I] (¶2) = appear, *turn out* (to be) [I] (¶2) = end up as, have a certain result; *rule out* [T] (¶3) = eliminate; *come in* [I] (¶5) = enter; *wait out* [T] (¶11) = wait until something (especially something bad) ends

Collocations: *surprise party* (¶3), *blood pressure* (¶4), *massive heart attack* (¶5), *no sign of* (¶11), *a broken heart* (¶12)

CHAPTER 12
The Dinner Party

Read *(page 86)*

Recycling Vocabulary

If students used *World of Reading 2*, ask them if they remember the following vocabulary items: *argue*, *insist*, and *scream*. Select words appropriate for your students, and call on volunteers to explain the meanings or provide them, if necessary. Tell students they will see these items in the reading, but they might have new meanings.

Refer to pages 7–8 ideas on how to review these words in meaningful activities.

LOCATION IN CHAPTER 12	LOCATION IN EARLIER CHAPTERS
crisis (¶3)	*crises:* "We often think of major crises such as natural disasters" (Chapter 9, ¶2)
exclaims (¶10)	*exclaimed:* "'It's wonderful!' Mama exclaimed." (Chapter 5, ¶12)
frighten (¶7)	*frightened:* "The housekeeper knew how frightened a little boy could be about going to school." (Chapter 4, line 25)
reaction (¶3)	*reaction:* "his initial alarm reaction may include fear of an accident" (Chapter 9, ¶5)
spirited (¶2)	*spirit:* "While my mother's spirit remained indomitable," (Chapter 5, ¶33)
striking (¶7)	*striking:* "There was a very striking connection" between stress and telomere length" (Chapter 11, Part 1, ¶7)

Vocabulary

Vocabulary Building: Using Paraphrases *(page 88)*

Remind students that paraphrasing complete ideas is one way that native speakers offer help; you might want to comment also that it takes time to develop the ability to paraphrase (even in one's first language) so they should practice regularly. They will need to develop this skill in order to write research papers in the university.

Vocabulary Reminder List

Phrasal verbs: *spring up* [I](¶2) = start quite suddenly; *come to* [I] (¶6) = become alert; *make for* [I] (¶9) = move toward; *ring out* [I] (¶9) = make a loud and clear sound/heard loud and clear; *light up* [T, I] (¶12) = show pleasure/satisfaction on

You might want to ask students if *looks up* in (¶6) (*he looks up at the rafters*) is a phrasal verb (it is not; *up* is an adverb showing where he looked). Have students contrast this with the phrase: *look up words in the dictionary*.

Collocations: *is what counts* (¶3) = is what is important; *comes over the face of* (¶4), *out of the corner of (his) eye* (¶9), *slam the door shut* (¶9), *just a minute* (¶11), *faint smile* (¶12)

Linking Readings

Once you complete Unit 3, you might want to have a class or group discussion on the following questions: 1. What is the relationship between exercise and stress? How do you think exercise works to reduce stress? (*exercise may help get your mind off negative thoughts, it increases endorphins and improves mood, it may relieve muscle tension*)
2. What, if any, connection do you see between the fact that there were more female subjects in the research reported in Chapter 11, Part 2 and the colonel's argument in Chapter 12?

Unit Wrap-Up

Word Families *(page 90)*

The following words in the Word Families in Unit 3 show a shift in primary stress. Draw students' attention to them.

abnorMALity	abNORmal (-ly)		
ENergy, ENergize	enerGETic (-ally)		
estiMAtion	EStimate (n.)	EStiMATE (v.)	EStiMATed
imMUNity	immuniZAtion	IMmunize	imMUNE
SEDative	seDAtion	seDATE	seDATed
tranQUILity	TRANquilizer	TRANquilize	TRANquil (-ly)

Note that *estimate* has a difference in the pronunciation of the noun (only the first syllable is clear—'Est∂mIt /) and the verb (the first and last syllables are clear /Est∂meIt/).

Polysemous Words

If you want to expand this exercise to include dictionary work, have students look up the meanings for these words in the sentences below.

1. *reaction*

    a. My first reaction to the speech is favorable. (*something you feel or do because of something that has happened*)

    b. I had a bad reaction to the medicine. (*physical change making you sick*)

    c. We are studying several chemical reactions in lab this week. (*change in two or more substances when they are mixed together*)

2. *tension*

    a. The air was filled with tension as the police confronted the striking workers. (*nervous or anxious feeling*)

    b. There is a lot of tension on this cable. (*tightness or stiffness*)

    c. Many women have to deal with the tension between work and family. (*difficult situation in which different needs or ideas affect the situation in opposite ways*)

    d. There is a great deal of tension between country X and country Y. (*feeling that exists when people/nations do not trust each other*)

3. *pace*

    a. Walk at a slow pace. (*rate or speed*)

    b. Mark off ten paces from the wall. (*steps*)

    c. We need a change of pace. (*a change in the way something is done or speed at which it's done*)

    d. It's sometimes hard to keep pace with changing times. (*move or change as fast as*)

    e. The professor paced back and forth in front of the classroom. (*move first in one direction, then in the other*)

Students might also enjoy pooling their knowledge of English to come up with both noun and verb uses for these words: *boost, dispute, estimate, pace, rate, recruit, release, sample, scream, strike, tip, trigger,* and *alert* (also *adj.*).

Recommended Readings and Websites

Redford, Gabrielle deGroot. "No-Worry Workouts." *AARP The Magazine*, May–June, 2009: 17.

    An article that links exercise to stress reduction, but suggests the need for walks to be longer than ten minutes.

Carmichael, Mary. "Who Says Stress is Bad for You?" *Newsweek*, February 23, 2009.

    One of several articles in this issue of *Newsweek* on the topic of stress.

Komaroff, Anthony L. "The Usual Suspect." *Newsweek*, February 23, 2009.

    A doctor's opinion that "the link between stress and disease has been oversold."

Thich Naht Hanh. "Washing Dishes." In *Peace Is Every Step*. New York: Bantam Books, a division of Bantam Doubleday Dell Publishing Group, Inc., 1991.

    How to make the ordinary task of washing dishes a relaxation technique.

For information on relaxation techniques and links to information about yoga and other systems: http://www.mayoclinic.com/health/relaxation-technique/sr00007.

UNIT 4: CULTURES IN CONTACT

Unit Opener (page 94)

As students discuss the questions and quote, you can write words related to the unit topic on the board, either those that students use correctly in the discussion or those that they need to learn. After the discussion, have students pronounce any new words and check to see that their meaning is clear. Offer definitions and example sentences as needed. Students will probably know most vocabulary needed to discuss the questions, but you might improve the discussion by teaching students words and expressions such as: *culture shock, disgust/ disgusted/disgusting, bewilderment/bewildered/bewildering, confusion/confused/confusing,* and *misunderstand/misunderstanding.*

CHAPTER 13
Culture

Read (page 95)

Recycling Vocabulary

If students used *World of Reading 2*, ask them if they remember the following vocabulary items: *behavior, bright* (intelligent), *enforce, environment, focus, public, restriction,* and *trade*. Select words appropriate for your students, and call on volunteers to explain the meanings or provide them, if necessary. Tell students they will see these items in the reading, but perhaps with new meanings.

Refer to pages 7–8 for ideas on how to review these words in meaningful activities.

LOCATION IN CHAPTER 13	LOCATION IN EARLIER CHAPTERS
a good deal of (¶3)	*a good deal of:* "Research has given us a good deal of knowledge about . . ." (Chapter 3, ¶1)
dumb (¶7)	*dumb:* "How can he (Mr. López) be so dumb?" (Chapter 6, ¶3)
humble (¶2)	*humble:* "Believing that he would feel less humble if he could sign his full name . . ." (Chapter 6, ¶9)
impressive (¶5)	*impressive:* "So far the results are very impressive." (Chapter 10, ¶12)
potentialities (¶9)	*potential:* "She (Mrs. Michelotti) . . . helped us reach our potential." (Chapter 5, ¶9) "He may become so conditioned to expect potential problems . . ." (Chapter 9, ¶5)
reaction (¶6)	*reaction:* "I found that the first reaction to sugar is enhanced energy" (Chapter 10, ¶9) "A woman's unfailing reaction in any crisis . . . is to scream." (Chapter 12, ¶3)
shame (¶8)	*shame:* "I (Hank) would feel a surge of resentment and shame." (Chapter 6, ¶3) *ashamed:* "Then maybe you won't be so ashamed of me." (Chapter 6, ¶15)

Vocabulary

Vocabulary Building *(page 98)*

Items 2 and 6: This exercise is divided unevenly to keep *legacy* and *heritage* in separate sections. Although these words refer to the same thing (that which is passed from one generation to the next), they have different collocations. A *legacy* is something the older generation leaves to the younger; a *heritage* is something the younger receives from the older.

Item 4, *abhorrent*: English seems to have quite a few words referring to extreme dislike; *abhor* is similar in strength to the verbs *despise* and *detest* in Chapter 4.

Item 7, *devilish*: Connect the meaning of this word to its root, *devil* or Satan, an evil spirit.

Item 9, *connotation*: *Connotations* for words can be both cultural and personal.

As an example of a likely cultural connotation, take the color red in English and Russian. To North Americans, red often connotes anger or embarrassment, though of course red is the favorite color of a lot of people. To a Russian, it tends to connote beauty; the Russian word for *beautiful* is related to the word for *red*. Ask students what connotations they have for other colors.

It takes a great deal of exposure to a second language to have personal connotations for words. If your group is sufficiently advanced, you might ask them which word in each group they would most and least like people to use to describe them and why. Use this frame:

He/She is a really _____ person.

Group 1: nice, kind, thoughtful, caring, pleasant, considerate, soft-hearted

Group 2: bright, brilliant, clever, intelligent, sharp, smart

Understanding the concept of connotation is important for both reading comprehension and writing because good writers choose words for both their denotations (dictionary meanings) and their connotations (what they suggest).

Item 10, *taboo*: This word, meaning "forbidden, prohibited" in English, was first recorded in 1777 in Captain James Cook's "A Voyage to the Pacific Ocean." Interestingly, related words appear in a number of Polynesian languages but in some they mean "sacred, holy" rather than "forbidden, prohibited."

Item 12, *crystalize*: The meaning of "form, take shape" is a metaphoric interpretation of the meaning in chemistry "to form crystals."

Vocabulary Reminder List

Phrasal verbs: *bring/brought up* [I] (¶1) = raise(d); *put on* [T] (¶3) = put clothing on your body

Collocations: *eat (his) fill* (¶6), *undergo* (¶9) *experiences*

Synonyms: *rear* (¶5), *raise* and *bring up* (¶1), *undergo/experience* (v.)

Text Analysis (page 100)

Students might comment that this selection has IBC organization. That is a good observation. Since this selection is a piece of a textbook chapter intended to define *culture*, you have the opportunity to comment that part of a whole can follow this organizational pattern; subtopics within a chapter need to be introduced, discussed, and concluded in some way before going on to the next subtopic. The conclusion of one subtopic is often also a transition to the next.

CHAPTER 14
Touching

Read (page 103)

Recycling Vocabulary

If students used *World of Reading 2*, ask them if they remember the following vocabulary items: *acquaintance, contact, crowd/crowded, distinct, homeland, lead to, manage, pray, public, purchase, scale, seek, signal,* and *unanimous*. Select words appropriate for your students, and call on volunteers to explain the meanings or provide them, if necessary. Tell students they will see these items in the reading, but perhaps with new meanings.

Refer to pages 7–8 for ideas on how to review these words in meaningful activities.

LOCATION IN CHAPTER 14	LOCATION IN EARLIER CHAPTERS
committed (¶3)	*committed:* "anger at the driver who committed the action" (Chapter 9, ¶5)
confronted (¶14)	*confrontation:* "Try cooperation instead of confrontation" (Chapter 9, ¶15)
connotations (¶11)	*connotation:* "To the Indian, the type of bodily contact involved in our social dancing has a directly sexual connotation." (Chapter 13, ¶8)
contradictions (¶9)	*contradicts:* "This finding, which contradicts the values that most people say they hold" (Chapter 3, ¶5)
furthermore (¶14)	*furthermore:* "Friends furthermore take care" (Chapter 1, ¶10) "Furthermore, the more similar others are, the more we like them." (Chapter 3, ¶4)
grabbed (¶9)	*grabbing:* "Then suddenly grabbing a can of furniture polish . . ." (Chapter 6, ¶13)
ignore (¶14)	*ignorance:* "His ignorance was almost too much for me to bear." (Chapter 6, ¶6)
jammed (¶12)	*jam:* "getting stuck in a traffic jam" (Chapter 9, ¶2)
point out (¶14)	*pointing out:* "She (Mrs. Michelotti) even served as tour guide, pointing out landmarks . . ." (Chapter 5, ¶18) *points out:* "Sharkey points out that heart tissue is rich in nerve endings" (Chapter 11, ¶8)
reaction (¶9, 14)	*reaction:* "a trader's wife in Arizona who took a somewhat devilish interest in producing a cultural reaction." (Chapter 13, ¶6)
screamed (¶7)	*screamed:* "I (Hank) twisted away and screamed at him" (Chapter 6, ¶13) *scream:* "A woman's unfailing reaction in any crisis . . . is to scream." (Chapter 12, ¶3)
sexual (¶8, 11); *homosexuality* (¶5)	*sexual:* "social dancing has a directly sexual connotation" (Chapter 13, ¶8)
somewhat (¶10)	*somewhat:* ". . . a trader's wife in Arizona who took a somewhat devilish interest in producing a cultural reaction." (Chapter 13, ¶6)

To help understand *uproar* (MMC) (¶7), students would benefit from knowing that *roar* is a continuous, loud noise or the sound of certain animals such as lions.

Comprehension Check

Second Reading *(page 106)*

Item 7: An observant student might point out that Liv Ullman comes from a non-touching country, which might lead to a discussion of how people can change cultural habits and how easy or difficult it is to do so.

Vocabulary

Vocabulary Building: Using Paraphrases *(page 107)*

There are some words with interesting origins in these exercises.

Item 2, *innocuous*: from the Latin *in-* (not) + *noxius* (poisonous, harmful, toxic)

Item 2, *misconstrue*: from the Latin *mis-* (wrongly) + *construe* (construct)

Item 4, *unanimous*: from the Latin *uno* (one) + *animus* (spirit) *of one spirit*

Item 5, *dilemma*: a Greek rhetorical term meaning having two (di-) propositions (lemma); there is an English saying "on the horns of a dilemma"

Item 9, *quintessential*: students may benefit from seeing *essential* in this word

Vocabulary Reminder List

Phrasal verbs: *pull away* [T, I] (¶3) = remove; *go up* [I] (¶12) = approach; *walk around* [I] (¶13) = walk without direction; *draw away* [I] (¶17) = pull away; *bend down* [I] (¶17) = lower the top of your body

In order to understand a writer's meaning, students must recognize the difference between a phrasal verb and a verb plus a prepositional phrase (answering the question *Where?*). Here are examples to discuss with students; the verb in one of the columns is from the reading.

PHRASAL VERB	VERB + PREPOSITION (ADVERBIAL PHRASE)
"Just go up and place your arm around him" (¶12)	I think you're going to have to go **up this hill** in first gear.
". . . each of us walks around in 'bubbles of personal space.'" (¶13)	We walked **around the block**.

Chapter-by-Chapter Teaching Tips   35

Collocations: *didn't have the faintest idea* (¶2), *hold hands* (¶5), *pay a visit to* (¶7), *make the first move* (¶7), *a surefire way to* (¶12), *and so it goes* (¶14) = and so it happens; *on behalf of* (¶17) = as a representative of

Text Analysis *(page 108)*

You might want to suggest that students ask themselves, "What does this example show? What is the writer illustrating with this anecdote?" Examples, especially anecdotes, can be very interesting in their own right, and readers can overlook their connection to the author's ideas and purposes.

CHAPTER 15
Change of Heart

Before You Read

Thinking about the Topic *(page 110)*

You might want to ask students to define the italicized vocabulary items (*get along, prejudice*). Remind them that they are target words.

Read *(page 110)*

Recycling Vocabulary

If students used *World of Reading 2*, ask them if they remember the following vocabulary items: *behavior, disappointment, guy, labor, minor, reason, regulation, signal, surface,* and *transform*. Select words appropriate for your students, and call on volunteers to explain the meanings or provide them, if necessary. Tell students they will see these items in the reading, but perhaps with new meanings.

Refer to pages 7–8 for ideas on how to review these words in meaningful activities.

LOCATION IN CHAPTER 15	LOCATION IN EARLIER CHAPTERS
accused (¶1)	accused: "teachers may be accused of molestation if they frequently hug, pat, or touch their students." (Chapter 14, ¶8)
annoyed (¶5)	annoyed: "'He wants you to cash it,' I added, annoyed by my father's use of the word cambiar." (Chapter 6, ¶10)
guilty (¶6)	guilt: "now guilt-ridden by what I had yelled at my dad" (Chapter 6, ¶15)
humbled (¶9)	humble: "Believing that he would feel less humble if he could sign his full name" (Chapter 6, ¶9) "A humble cooking pot is as much a cultural product as is a Beethoven sonata." (Chapter 13, ¶2)
irritated (¶5)	irritable: "If you are irritable and tense from lack of sleep" (Chapter 9, ¶11)
realm (¶2)	realms: "Marcus R. . . . loves online role-playing games—where he operates in 'realms' populated by thousands of other players." (Chapter 2, ¶3)
stubbornly (¶4)	stubborn: "personal problem, such as marital troubles or a stubborn weight problem." (Chapter 10, ¶10)
wanders (¶14)	wanderings: "the wanderings only you (my only mother) understand." (Chapter 8, ¶1)
wondered (¶8)	wondered: "I (Joseph Michelotti) wondered who had come to see me at that hour." (Chapter 5, ¶32) wondering: "I've mulled that signature over and over, wondering what you meant." (Chapter 8, ¶8)

The word *fortressed* (MMC) (¶4) is used metaphorically. A fortress (primarily a military term) is a large, strong building used for defending an important place. Ask students what ideas the writer may be conveying about the way the author lived in her pink Spanish house.

Surmising (MMC) (¶7) is a formal word and includes the idea that your guess is based on information that you already know.

The extreme sadness called *grief* (MMC) (¶8) is most often associated with the death of someone you love.

Vocabulary

Vocabulary Building *(page 113)*

Item 4, *stereotype*: Your students might be interested to know that this word was originally a French printing term dating from 1798, meaning, "printing from a solid plate of type." In 1850 the meaning, "image perpetuated without change," is recorded; the modern meaning of an unfair idea of a person or group based on preconceived notions dates from 1922.

Item 6, *assimilate*: Students will benefit from seeing the word *similar* in this word. To *assimilate* means "to become part of a new group and be accepted by that group," which usually involves becoming more similar in certain ways.

Item 7, *rationalize*: Students should benefit from making the connection between *rational* and *reason*. A rational person is one who uses reason; to *rationalize* is to find or invent reasonable explanations for something (especially something you probably shouldn't be doing).

Item 9, *anchors*: Ask students if they know what an *anchor* on a boat is. Then ask them to paraphrase what the author means by her *anchors*.

Item 11, *biases*: *Biases* is used here as a close synonym of *prejudices*. Learning to recognize that a writer has a *bias* or tends to favor some group or point of view (and learning to be objective and *unbiased* in speaking and writing) are important academic goals. *Bias* tends to collocate with more intellectual activities (bias in writing) and *prejudice* with more emotional ones (racial or gender prejudice).

You might ask students whether they see any kind of bias in the writing for the readings they have done in *World of Reading 3*. For example, does the writer show any bias in favor of or against making friends on the Internet in "Online Friendships" from Chapter 2?

Vocabulary Reminder List

Phrasal Verbs: *get along (with)* [T, I] (subhead, ¶1) = have good relationships with; *shout back* [I] (¶2) = return a shout; *take out* [T] (¶4) = put outside; *pass by* [I] (¶4) = walked/drove past; *wake up* [T, I] (¶6) = become/make awake; *cut off* [T] (¶6) = remove by cutting

Collocations: *know/knew what I am/was talking about* (¶2), *bring/brought (something) to the surface* (¶3), *have (nothing) in common* (¶4), *restore peace* (¶6), *put a stop to (something)* (¶7), *it is/was (something) I can/could live with* (¶7), *bring (someone) into compliance with (something)* (¶7), *made (someone) out to be* (¶9)

Compound Adjectives: *six-figure* job (¶8), *hard-working* people (¶9)

Word Analysis: The word *bill* once commonly meant "advertisement," hence *billboard* (¶5), a place for announcements.

Text Analysis *(page 114)*

Additional Discussion: Unified writing

After students have completed the exercise, you might want to do another text analysis activity. Put the words *unity* and the phrase *unified writing* on the board. Ask for their definitions and write them on the board. (Both terms refer to the "oneness" or "wholeness" of the writing, the fact that it deals with one topic; there are no sentences or paragraphs that are not related to that topic.) Discuss these questions with students to reveal the unity of this essay:

- What is the topic of this essay? (*a person's change of heart about her immigrant neighbors*)
- What does Rodney King have to do with the topic? (*His case is used to introduce the topic of prejudice and lead the writer to talk about her own situation and her prejudice toward her neighbors in ¶2–7.*)
- What does she write about in ¶8? (*the events that caused her change of heart*)
- What does the content of ¶9–12 provide? (*examples of things she learned about her neighbors and their relationship now*)
- How do ¶13–14 help to unify the essay? (*Her concluding thoughts refer back to things mentioned earlier—Rodney King and the rooster.*)
- Is there any sentence that doesn't relate to the topic of her change of heart? (*Answers will vary.*)

CHAPTER 16
Assembly Line

Read (*page 115*)

Recycling Vocabulary

If students used *World of Reading 2*, ask them if they remember the following vocabulary items: *absolutely, achievement, actually, ambition, apparently, argue, behavior, better suited to, chance, contract, curiosity, deal (n.), district, equivalent, expect, expert, find out, flexible, give up, guy, labor, miracle, nasty, nervous, perceive, satisfied, scores of, single, solely, track/tracking, urban, venture,* and *wares*. Select words appropriate for your students, and call on volunteers to explain the meanings or provide them, if necessary. Tell students they will see these items in the reading, but perhaps with new meanings.

Refer to pages 7–8 for ideas on how to review these words in meaningful activities.

LOCATION IN CHAPTER 16	LOCATION IN EARLIER CHAPTERS
accomplished (¶6), *accomplish* (¶6)	*accomplishments*: "praising even our most ordinary accomplishments" (Chapter 5, ¶12)
	accomplish: "Trying to take care of everything at once can seem overwhelming, and, as a result, you may not accomplish anything." (Chapter 9, ¶14)
amazing (¶6)	*amazed*: "She (Amy) was amazed that he (Jim) wasn't changed" (Chapter 4, line 72)
attractive (¶6)	*physical attractiveness* (Chapter 3, ¶5)
	attraction "the literature on interpersonal attraction" (Chapter 3, ¶2)
	attract "it (folk wisdom) also maintains that opposites attract." (Chapter 3, ¶4)
	attractive "physically attractive people are more popular" (Chapter 3, ¶5)

(*continued*)

LOCATION IN CHAPTER 16	LOCATION IN EARLIER CHAPTERS
ceased (¶88)	*cease:* "cells cease dividing and soon die." (Chapter 11, Part 1, ¶2)
convinced (¶25)	*convince:* "I tried to convince him (José) that . . . we wanted our children to do something better than we did" (Chapter 7, ¶13)
crazy (¶62)	*craziness:* "'What craziness is it this time?' my husband asks." (Chapter 8, ¶6)
degree (¶5)	*degree:* "the increased energy from walking was still present to a small degree." (Chapter 10, ¶7)
desperation (¶62), desperate (¶87)	*desperately:* "young people desperately need community" (Chapter 2, ¶5)
	desperate: "'Tutti-frutti,' she (Hannah) said with desperate haste." (Chapter 4, line 121)
eventually (¶73)	*eventually:* "Eventually, he did learn to write two words" (Chapter 6, ¶9)
	"The sugar . . . eventually caused fatigue. (Chapter 10, ¶9)
excited (¶37)	*excited:* "it can be easy to get excited and 'sound too mean' about somebody in an IM" (Chapter 2, ¶11)
	unexciting: "Without stress, life would be dull and unexciting." (Chapter 9, ¶1)
forever (¶1)	*forever:* "teens plan to stay connected to their friends through college—and maybe forever." (Chapter 2, ¶19)
frank (¶35)	*frankness:* "qualities most valued in a friend . . . followed closely by supportiveness, frankness, and a sense of humor" (Chapter 3, ¶6)
grasp (¶15, 66)	*grasp:* "words . . . seemed confusing and totally beyond his grasp when they appeared in print or in my mother's handwriting." (Chapter 6, ¶16)
ignored (¶16)	*ignorance:* "His ignorance was almost too much for me to bear." (Chapter 6, ¶6)
	ignore: "they accept body contact or just seem to ignore it by 'retreating within themselves.'" (Chapter 14, ¶14 second bullet)
promoter (¶20)	*promotes:* "Discovering that others have similar attitudes, values, or traits promotes our liking for them." (Chapter 3, ¶4)

LOCATION IN CHAPTER 16	LOCATION IN EARLIER CHAPTERS
shrugged (¶30)	*shrugged:* "he (José) shrugged and held up his hands, as if he hadn't quite made up his mind about whose dream it was." (Chapter 7, ¶17)
struck (¶36)	*striking:* "There was a very striking connection" between stress and telomere length" (Chapter 11, Part 1, ¶7) "the commotion would frighten the cobra into striking." (Chapter 8, ¶7)
trace (n.) (¶23)	*trace:* "Why do some nations trace descent through the father" (Chapter 13, ¶1)
utter (¶96)	*utterly:* "She was amazed that he wasn't changed, that he wasn't hurt, or perhaps utterly unalive, murdered." (Chapter 4, line 73)
wonder (¶19, 87)	*wondering:* "I've mulled that signature over and over, wondering what you meant. (Chapter 8, ¶8) *wondered:* "I wondered how—or if—I would be able to pull myself out." (Chapter 15, ¶8)
yelled (¶62)	*yelled:* "now guilt-ridden by what I had yelled at my dad" (Chapter 6, ¶15)

This is a long story with a fairly difficult beginning but with considerable predictability once the reader gets into it. Therefore, we recommend that students read at least ¶1–6 in class, which introduces them to the characters and the setting. You might want to further divide Part 1 as follows:

(¶7–15): how the Indian is treated in his culture

(¶16–24): Mr. Winthrop's first conversation with the Indian

(¶24–44): Mr. Winthrop's return to New York and his deal with Mr. Kemple

Questions before Part 2:

1. He cleverly gets Mr. Kemple to raise an already-good price. Mr. Winthrop seems smart in his own culture when he deals with Mr. Kemple.
2. Answers will vary, but students might be able to predict that Mr. Winthrop's lack of understanding of the Indian's culture and his artistic point of view will mean that he will not act intelligently in his negotiation with the Indian.

Nooyorg (¶25) is an alternative spelling of "New York" to suggest a strange pronunciation perhaps suggesting that the author is making fun of Mr. Winthrop.

Note that *come out with the salad* (¶70), referring to *money*, is a nonessential expression here since Winthrop also asks, "What is the price?"

Vocabulary

Vocabulary Reminder List

Phrasal verbs: *turn to* [I] (¶2) = begin again to think about, return to a topic

Collocations: *the beaten track* (¶2), *there was nothing else for him to do* (¶5), *at heart* (¶6), *serve certain purposes* ¶7), *pay outright* (¶9), *prospective buyer* (¶9), *ought to be ashamed* (¶9), *it's your lucky day* (¶9), *Now what do you think of that?* (¶10), *little if any knowledge* of *the outside world* (¶11)

Text Analysis *(page 127)*

Additional Discussion: The Writer's Point of View

Understanding the writer's point of view in this story requires seeing several comments as "tongue-in-cheek," that is, as jokes, though they might appear serious. How does each of the following sections or sentences reveal the author's true feelings?

(¶1–2): The phrase "the glorious mission on earth" sounds a bit sarcastic and we understand that Traven doesn't value the promotion of capitalism in Mexico. He has negative feelings about capitalists who think their way is the only way and wish to impose it on other parts of the world. Also sounding a bit sarcastic is the phrase "and indulge in his new avocation" (*hobby*).

(¶25): "After three weeks' stay," Mr. Winthrop knows everything. Since this is obviously not possible, we get the idea that Traven is making fun of the man who thinks he knows everything.

(¶46): "Come to think of it, that Republic isn't so backward after all." Traven is showing Mr. Winthrop to be a person whose judgment of Mexico is influenced by the profit he might make.

(¶98): "American garbage cans escaped the fate of receiving the art and soul of the Indian." In these words, Traven reveals that he values the Indian's works of art which he believes would not have been appreciated in the United States.

Linking Readings

Once you complete Unit 4, you might want to have a class or group discussion on the following questions: 1. Readings 2, 3, and 4 all deal with what can happen when people do not understand the meaning of gestures or actions in another culture. Summarize the aspects of a culture that these readings show may be hard to understand. 2. What, if anything, can get people to leave their comfort zone and try to understand how people from a different culture view the world? 3. These readings show cross-cultural bias, prejudice, or stereotyping. Which, if any, have you experienced and how did you deal with them?

Unit Wrap-Up

Word Families *(page 128)*

The following words in the Word Families in Unit 4 show a shift in primary stress. Draw students' attention to them.

confrontTAion / -al	conFRONT
HARmony, HARmonize	harMOnious (-ly)
hesiTAtion	HESitate, HESitant (-ly)
indigNAtion	inDIGnant (-ly)

Note the change in the pronunciation of the second vowel in *collide* /aɪ/ and *collision* [ɪ].

Recommended Readings

Cofer, Judith Ortiz. "Don't Misread My Signals." In *The Latin Deli: Prose and Poetry.* Athens: University of Georgia Press, 1993.

    Personal essay with examples of stereotyping of Latinas.

Divakaruni, Chitra Banerjee. "Yuba City School." In *Black Candle.* Calyx Books, 1991.

(and in)

Building on Basics. White Plains: Addison-Wesley Longman, 1999.

    Poem about the suffering of a Sikh schoolboy in northern California from the mother's point of view.

Saroyan, William. "The Peasant." In *The Man With The Heart in the Highlands and other early stories (A revived modern classic).* New York: New Directions, 1992.

    The story of a successful immigrant who was never completely happy in his new country and always missed his village in Armenia.

Tan, Amy. "Double Face." In *The Joy Luck Club.* New York: Ivy Books published by Ballantine Books, a division of Random House, 1989.

    A mother's thoughts on her daughter's acculturation in the United States.

UNIT 5 ETHICS

Unit Opener (page 131)

As students discuss the questions and quotes, you can write words related to the unit topic on the board, either those that students use correctly in the discussion or those that they need to learn. After the discussion, have students pronounce any new words and check to see that their meaning is clear. Offer definitions and example sentences as needed. Students will probably know most vocabulary needed to discuss the questions, but you might improve the discussion by teaching students words and expressions such as: *confidential information, copyright, dilemma, plagiarism,* and *unethical.*

CHAPTER 17
Treasures from Troy: An Introduction to Ethics

Read (page 133)

Recycling Vocabulary

If students used *World of Reading 2*, ask them if they remember the following vocabulary items: *access, actually, apparently, behavior, compete/competitive/competition, concerned, conduct, deal, engineer, expect, issues, professional, public, raise,* and *trade*. Select words appropriate for your students, and call on volunteers to explain the meanings or provide them, if necessary. Tell students they will see these items in the reading, but perhaps with new meanings.

44 *World of Reading 3 Teacher's Manual*

Refer to pages 7–8 for ideas on how to review these words in meaningful activities.

LOCATION IN CHAPTER 17	LOCATION IN EARLIER CHAPTERS
caution (¶1)	*cautious:* "teens need to be cautious even when they think they're talking to their real-life friends." (Chapter 2, ¶15)
furthermore (¶7)	*furthermore:* "Friends furthermore take care" (Chapter 1, ¶10) "And furthermore, they (Korean shopkeepers) won't look me in the eyes." (Chapter 14, ¶10)
impacts (¶5)	*impact:* "you can prevent some distress as well as minimize its impact." (Chapter 9, ¶6)
obligation (¶1)	*obligations:* "intimate friendships involve important rights and obligations." (Chapter 1, ¶10)
reflecting on (¶6)	*reflects on:* "Everything you do reflects on the family" (Chapter 5, ¶24)

You might want to review synonyms for *horrified* (MMC) (¶8), showing that it is probably stronger than the others they have seen in this book (*surprised, amazed, shocked, horrified*).

Comprehension Check

First Reading *(page 135)*

You might want to begin by asking students what kinds of situations call for the application or use of ethics (¶1).

Second Reading *(page 136)*

The two Comprehension Checks overlap in part; however, the True/False items encourage students to examine the basis for making decisions more carefully.

Vocabulary

Vocabulary Building *(page 136)*

Item 2, *controversy*: Like *contradict/contradiction*, which students saw in Chapters 3 and 14, this word comes from Latin and contains *contra-* (against) + *versus* (turn). In a *controversy*, there are opposing ideas; one "turned against the other."

Vocabulary Reminder List

Phrasal verbs: *look up* [T] (¶8) = find in a textbook/reference book; *go out* [I] (¶8) = leave home to do something; *pick up* [T] (¶8) = get, take, buy; *go back* [I] (¶10) = return

Notice that *look on* in the first line of (¶8) is not a phrasal verb but a verb + a prepositional phrase beginning with *on* (*on the front page*).

Collocations: *as* (name) *puts it* (¶1), *keep quiet about* (it) (¶4), *for starters* (¶4), *decision-making process* (¶5), *in the spotlight of public opinion* (¶5), *get things started* (¶6), *out in(to) the open* (¶6), *ahead of time* (¶7), *raises ethical problems* (¶7), *get a good night's sleep* (¶8), *it's* (your) *turn* (¶10)

CHAPTER 18

Why You Shouldn't Do It

Read *(page 140)*

Recycling Vocabulary

If students used *World of Reading 2*, ask them if they remember the following vocabulary items: *argue, behavior, compete/competitive/competition, contrary to, engineer, major, public, track/tracking,* and *undertake*. Select words appropriate for your students, and call on volunteers to explain the meanings or provide them, if necessary. Tell students they will see these items in the reading, but perhaps with new meanings.

Refer to pages 7–8 for ideas on how to review these words in meaningful activities.

LOCATION IN CHAPTER 18	LOCATION IN EARLIER CHAPTERS
commitment (¶7)	*committed:* "anger at the driver who committed the action" (Chapter 9, ¶5) "I could have committed a Sahara-sized *faux pas*." (Chapter 14, ¶3)
distribute (¶1, 5), *distributions* (¶4)	*distributed:* " they . . . found the exam, downloaded it, and distributed copies to their friends" (Chapter 17, ¶3)
ensure (Thinking about the Topic)	*ensure:* "to ensure that the mood shift was not due simply to a stroll through the attractive campus surroundings." (Chapter 10, ¶5)
establishing (¶11), *established* (¶13)	*established:* "we established the following categories of friendship:" (Chapter 1, ¶2) "one of the more firmly established findings in the literature on interpersonal attraction" (Chapter 3, ¶2)
exclusive (¶4)	*exclusively:* "there would be time enough once he (Mr. Kemple) knew the price and whether he could get a whole load exclusively." (Chapter 16, ¶29) *exclusive:* "I'm (Mr. Winthrop) selling to the highest bidder, on an exclusive basis" (Chapter 16, ¶33)
exposure (¶11)	*expose:* "although we may not expose as much . . . to each of our closest friends," (Chapter 1, ¶9) *exposure:* "repeated exposure to any stimulus . . . usually makes us like the stimulus more." (Chapter 3, ¶3)
peer (¶1)	*peer:* "children rating their peers' popularity on the basis of attractiveness" (Chapter 3, ¶5)
promote (¶4)	*promotes:* "knowing that someone evaluates us positively promotes our attraction to that person." (Chapter 3, ¶4)
rationalize (¶5), *rationalization* (¶9)	*rationalized:* "but rationalized it (the death of the rooster) as being necessary to restore peace and quiet to the neighborhood." (Chapter 15, ¶6)

LOCATION IN CHAPTER 18	LOCATION IN EARLIER CHAPTERS
resources (¶12)	*resources:* "the body depletes its resources for fighting stress." (Chapter 9, ¶5)
soul (¶7)	*soul:* "with bits of my soul woven into them." (Chapter 16, ¶97)
strive (¶7)	*striving:* "You will find satisfaction in just *being*, without striving." (Chapter 9, ¶19)
virtually (¶2)	*virtually:* "repeated exposure to any stimulus . . . virtually anything—usually makes us like the stimulus more." (Chapter 3, ¶3)
warehousemen (¶13)	*wares:* "At the market he (the Indian) had to pay twenty centavos in taxes to sell his wares." (Chapter 16, ¶9)

Vocabulary

Vocabulary Building: Synonyms *(page 143)*

Item 1, *burn*: You may want to comment that *burn*, like *download* in ¶10–11, is an example of technical jargon: words, acronyms, and expressions used in a specific field. When people begin to work in a field, they must learn the technical jargon. Students can probably give you many more examples of computer technical jargon: *FAQs, favorites, homepage, jpg (jpeg), link, server, streaming,* etc.

Item 6, *betrays*: When a person *betrays* another, he or she is breaking a relationship of trust, so *be unfair to* is a weak synonym of *betray*.

Items 11 and 12: The words *undertaking* and *resources* are quite general in their meaning. *Undertaking* refers to an important job or activity, usually complicated. A *resource* is something that can be used to do something (*natural resources*: petroleum, gas, trees, the sun) or can refer to personal strengths (her personality is a great *resource*). The synonyms given here reflect the specific context of this reading.

Vocabulary Reminder List

Phrasal verbs: *check out* [T] (¶11) = check, with an especially informal tone

Collocations: *hold the copyright* (¶1), *contrary to what some people would/will say/tell you* (¶2), *it is against the law to* (¶4), *is about* verb+ing/noun (¶7), *tell that to . . .* (¶9), *(one) out of every (ten)* (¶10), *decide for yourself* (¶11), *all over (the Internet)* (¶11)

Verb + preposition: *belong to* (¶1)

Text Analysis

Author's Purpose *(page 146)*

As an additional activity, you might ask students to discuss the following question: How do you know that the author's purpose is to persuade? In other words, what are some characteristics of persuasive writing?

- the opening sentence suggests that people are doing something illegal, and ends with the strong claim, "you are stealing"
- the use of the word *shouldn't* in the title and in ¶3
- the building of an argument; the stating and numbering of reasons intended to convince the reader not to illegally download music
- statements correcting common misinterpretations, including rationalizations for illegal downloading (¶5, 9), what music is really about (¶7), what gives music its value (¶7), and the real victims of this supposedly 'victimless' crime (¶9, 10, 13)
- looking at the situation from another point of view (¶11), but showing the limit to that other point of view

CHAPTER 19
A Plea for the Chimps

Before You Read

Thinking about the Topic *(page 147)*

Check that students can define *primate*, *cure*, and *vaccine*, since this is particularly relevant vocabulary for this reading.

Read *(page 148)*

Recycling Vocabulary

If students used *World of Reading 2*, ask them if they remember the following vocabulary items: *absolutely, actually, argue, behavior, capable of, capacity, casual, compatible, contact, contract, curiosity, decent, dedication, determined/determine/determination, dialogue, distinct, elaborate, enable, endure/ endurance, environment, equipped, expect, facilities, identical, intention, issue, lead to, maintain, major, model, prompt (someone) to, public, quit, reason, regulation, rewarding/reward, sensitive, set up, single, sort, unexpected,* and *unique*. Select words appropriate for your students, and call on volunteers to explain the meanings or provide them, if necessary. Tell students they will see these items in the reading, but perhaps with new meanings.

Refer to pages 7–8 for ideas on how to review these words in meaningful activities.

LOCATION IN CHAPTER 19	LOCATION IN EARLIER CHAPTERS
alternatives (¶4)	alternative: "this alternative looks poor when seen from the standpoints of the other students and the teacher" (Chapter 17, ¶9)
boredom (¶42)	bored: "One way to keep from getting bored, sad, and lonely is . . ." (Chapter 9, ¶13)
	boring: "he was about to attend a long and boring lecture" (Chapter 10, ¶1)
briefly (¶13)	brief: "Your scrawled message, as always, is brief" (Chapter 8, ¶5)
companions (¶17, 23, 40)	companionship: "how a woman could be so selfish and so undesirous of feminine companionship in the home" (Chapter 13, ¶4)
currently (¶5, update line 6)	currently: "She is currently working on a book about teens' strong need for connection with others." (Chapter 2, ¶5)
	current: "talking to us about history, politics and current events" (Chapter 5, ¶17)
depressed (¶41)	depressed: "talk about being overweight but not about being depressed." (Chapter 1, ¶4)
despair (¶3, 9, 14)	despair: "Mr. Winthrop shouted at the poor Indian in utter despair" (Chapter 16, ¶96)
enriching (¶42)	enrich: "they (friends) enrich the quality of our emotional life." (Chapter 1, ¶1)
established (¶36, update line 10)	established: "established the following categories of friendship" (Chapter 1, ¶2)
	"Songwriters and artists, whether established or up-and-coming" (Chapter 18, ¶13)
excited (¶18)	unexciting: "Without stress, life would be dull and unexciting." (Chapter 9, ¶1)
	excited: "All right, all right, no reason to get excited, no reason at all." (Chapter 16, ¶37)
forever (¶14)	forever: "teens plan to stay connected to their friends through college—and maybe forever." (Chapter 2, ¶19)
	"Lions, who are forever conscious of their glorious mission on earth." (Chapter 16, ¶1)
frightened (¶17)	frighten: "the commotion would frighten the cobra into striking." (Chapter 12, ¶7)
a great deal of (¶44)	a good deal of: "Research has given us a good deal of knowledge about" (Chapter 3, ¶1)
	"A good deal of human behavior can be understood . . . if" (Chapter 13, ¶3)

(continued)

LOCATION IN CHAPTER 19	LOCATION IN EARLIER CHAPTERS
infant (¶14, 25)	infancy: "Orphaned in infancy, he was reared in a remote village." (Chapter 13, ¶5)
infect(ed) (¶5, 11, 26), infection (¶33, 40, 41)	infectious: "Her (Mother's) confidence in us was infectious" (Chapter 5, ¶15)
insane (¶11)	insane: "Mr. Winthrop felt as if he would go insane any minute now." (Chapter 16, ¶79)
isolation (¶12)	isolated: "Mama . . . traded her busy city neighborhood for a more isolated life." (Chapter 5, ¶8)
landmark (update line 11)	landmark: "pointing out landmarks and recounting local history." (Chapter 5, ¶18)
manipulate (¶42)	manipulate: "This means avoiding actions which deceive, manipulate, or force someone to do something." (Chapter 17, ¶9 chart)
miserable (¶26, 46)	miserable: "this miserable Indian village" (Chapter 16, ¶20)
nature (¶5, 15, 16, 46)	nature: "All this does not mean that there is no such thing as raw human nature." (Chapter 13, ¶9)
	"(Ethics) creates theories about the nature of right and wrong," (Chapter 17, ¶1)
obligatory (¶42)	obligations: "intimate friendships involve important rights and obligations." (Chapter 1, ¶10)
	"(Ethics) creates theories about the nature of right and wrong, duty, obligation, freedom, virtue, and other issues" (Chapter 17, ¶1)
potential (¶6)	potential: "She heightened our self-esteem and helped us reach our potential." (Chapter 5, ¶9)
	"He may become so conditioned to expect potential problems when he drives" (Chapter 9, ¶5)
rage (¶21)	rage: "mad but not blind with rage" (Chapter 1, ¶4)
	"even if they've (the postcards) driven me to tears or rage" (Chapter 8, ¶15)
reassuringly (¶22), reassurance (¶17)	reassure: "Indeed, we will frequently turn—for reassurance . . . to friends" (Chapter 1, ¶10)
resemblances (¶2)	resembled: "cells from the highly stressed women resembled cells of low-stressed volunteers who were 10 years older." (Chapter 11, ¶7)
restricting (¶31)	restrict: "to wish to restrict her husband to one mate." (Chapter 13, ¶4)

LOCATION IN CHAPTER 19	LOCATION IN EARLIER CHAPTERS
similarities (¶1, 2, 41), *similar* (¶21)	*Similarity/similar:* "One reason similarity increases the likelihood of interpersonal attraction is that we assume that people with similar attitudes will evaluate us positively" (Chapter 3, ¶4) "The immediate mood change from the candy bar was similar to the effect of walking: increased energy." (Chapter 10, ¶8)
stimulating (¶42)	*stimulate:* "nerve endings that can stimulate the release of catecholamines" (Chapter 11, Part 2, ¶8)
striking (¶2)	*striking:* "'There was a very striking connection' between stress and telomere length" (Chapter 11, Part 1, ¶7) "the commotion would frighten the cobra into striking." (Chapter 12, ¶7)
utterly (¶14)	*utterly:* "or perhaps utterly unalive, murdered." (Chapter 4, line 73) *utter:* "Mr. Winthrop shouted at the poor Indian in utter despair," (Chapter 16, ¶96)
victims (¶28)	*victimless:* "Another rationalization for stealing music is that illegal copying is a victimless crime" (Chapter 18, ¶9)
well-being (¶17)	*well-being:* "Play can be just as important to your well-being as work" (Chapter 9, ¶12) "But making music is also about career and financial well-being." (Chapter 18, ¶7)

Students may benefit if you connect the word *haunted* (MMC) to ghosts that some people believe haunt us or our houses.

Students may be able to relate the word *captive* (MMC) to *capture*.

Comprehension Check *(page 154)*

There is only one comprehension check for this article because the Text Analysis exercise provides a second opportunity to understand the major points in Goodall's argument.

Vocabulary

Vocabulary Building *(page 155)*

Item 1, *justified*: Relate *justified* to the meaning of *just* = fair, right.

Item 2, *despair*: *Despair* is a strong word; it refers to a condition when all hope is gone.

Item 10, *empathy*: *Empathy* and *sympathy* are close in meaning. Both refer to the ability to understand the feelings and problems of others. However, only *sympathy* can be paraphrased by *feel sorry for*. *Empathy* suggests that the person can feel the same feelings as the one who is suffering, usually because they have lived through the same experiences.

Item 15, *compatible*: You might help students remember the meaning of this word if they discuss what is meant by *compatible people* and *compatible equipment*.

Item 16, *prone to*: *Prone to* tends to collocate with negative things, such as *disease, fits of anger,* and *eating problems;* an area can be *prone to flooding, hurricanes,* etc. This word suggests the bad things are likely or somewhat frequent.

Item 17, *prey to*: *Prey to* also collocates with negatives (*prey* is the animal that another animal hunts for food), but it does not suggest frequency.

Vocabulary Reminder List

Phrasal verbs: *give up* [I] (¶14) = stop trying; *break into* [T-not separable] (¶18) = to suddenly start doing something; *bring up* [T] (¶22) = raise/rear the young; *put away* [T] (¶22) = put something where it is usually kept; *switch on* [T] (¶22) = turn on, start; *let out* [T] (¶26) = release; *set up* [T] (¶28) = create; *stay on* [I] (¶29) = continue, don't leave; *lie about/around* [I] (¶32) = scattered; *pass on* [T] (¶40) = give to someone else; *bring about* [T] (¶45) = make happen, cause; *bring together* [T] (¶45) = bring to a meeting, unite; *speak out for* (¶46) = be the voice of

Collocations: *in the long run* (¶3), *steps in this direction* (¶3), (There is) *growing public awareness of* (¶3), *Let us . . . consider a more important issue* (¶7), *stressed beyond endurance* (¶14), *a sense of humor* (¶21), *come to accept* (¶29), *stand firm* (¶30), *uphold high standards* (¶30), *It is known that* (¶41), *give (someone) a better deal* (¶44)

Verb + preposition: *depend on* (¶3), *cater to* (¶24), *equip with* (¶28), *inflict on* (¶28)

Text Analysis (page 157)

When students have finished this exercise, ask them to look at their results, trace the steps in Goodall's argument, and evaluate it. Ask them to think about which arguments are more or less convincing to them. The following list outlines her argument:

- After stating her topic, she asks the question she thinks is really important: *Should chimpanzees be used in laboratory research?*

- Then, she focuses on another question that she believes she can answer convincingly: *How are we treating chimpanzees in research laboratories?*

- She paints the picture of the conditions and treatment in laboratories where conditions are particularly bad.

- She shows how those conditions and treatment go against the nature of chimpanzees in the wild (to convince us of how much they must be suffering).

- She discusses the complicated issue of human responsibility in letting these conditions and treatment continue (suggesting that though it is not easy to resolve the problem, humans are the only ones who can do anything).

- She discusses changes that can be made to make the situation better.

- She presents hopeful signs, thus ending on a more positive note.

- She reminds her audience indirectly that the animals are our responsibility when she says that she speaks for them since they cannot speak for themselves.

CHAPTER 20

The Wallet

Read *(page 159)*

Recycling Vocabulary

If students used *World of Reading 2*, ask them if they remember the following vocabulary items: *awkward, cute, raise,* and *track*. Select words appropriate for your students, and call on volunteers to explain the meanings or provide them, if necessary. Tell students they will see these items in the reading, but perhaps with new meanings.

Refer to pages 7–8 for ideas on how to review these words in meaningful activities.

LOCATION IN CHAPTER 20	LOCATION IN EARLIER CHAPTERS
annoying (¶3)	*annoyed*: "I (Hank) added, annoyed by my father's use of the word *cambiar*." (Chapter 6, ¶10)
	"I was annoyed when Hispanic salespeople in Radio Shack didn't understand when I asked for lithium batteries or extension cords." (Chapter 15, ¶5)
boredom (¶3)	*boredom*: "A variety of simple devices designed to alleviate boredom could be produced quite cheaply." (Chapter 19, ¶42)
deliberately (¶1)	*deliberate on*: "So these tests help you to cover all the ethics bases when you deliberate on what you should do." (Chapter 17, ¶9)
despairingly (¶2)	*despair*: "chimpanzees sat huddled, far gone in depression and despair." (Chapter 19, ¶9)
grab (¶3)	*grabbing*: "Then suddenly grabbing a can of furniture polish," (Chapter 6, ¶13)
	grabbed: "if, God forbid, he grabbed my knee, I would punch him in the nose." (Chapter 14, ¶9)
lingering (¶2)	*linger*: "an innocuous touch on someone's hand or arm can be misconstrued as a sexual move, especially if we let it linger." (Chapter 14, ¶8)
roared (¶4)	*uproar*: "The reason behind that uproar was that . . . no one touches the Queen." (Chapter 14, ¶7)
	roar: "All she (a chimp) could hear was the incessant roar of air rushing through vents into her prison." (Chapter 19, ¶12)
shift (¶2)	*shift*: "to ensure that the mood shift was not due simply to a stroll through the attractive campus surroundings." (Chapter 10, ¶5)
stare (¶7) (n.)	*stared*: "Mama called the youngsters to our door, where they stared greedily at a pot of steaming homemade soup" (Chapter 5, ¶29)

Vocabulary

Vocabulary Reminder List

Phrasal verbs: *come back* [I] (¶1) = return; *sweated out* [T] (¶2) = given off drops of water; *lined up* [T] (¶2) = placed in a line; *turn around* [I] (¶2) = face the other way; *look away* [I] (¶7) = look in the other direction; *go on* [I] (¶8) = continue; *speed away* [I] (¶9) = drive off fast

Collocations: *looking (her) up and down* (¶2) = looking from head to foot; *in a row* (¶3) = one after the other; *keep track* (¶3) = keep count

Linking Readings

Once you complete Unit 5, you might want to have a class or group discussion on the following question: What similarities and differences do you notice in the way the arguments are presented to readers in "Why You Shouldn't Do It" (Chapter 18) and "A Plea for the Chimps" (Chapter 19)? Discuss the following:

- the media for which the articles were written (website, newspaper magazine)
- the topic—that is—the ease or difficulty of what the writer wants to accomplish
- the number of arguments, amount of repetition, amount of detail, and style of writing

As of May, 2009, "Why You Shouldn't Do It" was available for students to see the layout at: http://www.musicunited.org/4_shouldntdoit.html.

Unit Wrap-Up

Word Families *(page 164)*

The following words in the Word Families in Unit 5 show a shift in primary stress. Draw students' attention to them.

appreciAtion	apPREciate, apPREciative (-ly)
CONtroversy	controVERsial
delibERAtion	*deLIBerATE *deLIBerate (-ly)
isoLAtion	Isolate, Isolated
rationaliZAtion	RAtionalize

* The final syllable of the verb is /eɪ/; of the adjective and adverb /ɪt/

You may want to show the word families for two other words in this unit, *captive* and *justify*, and have students choose the word that correctly completes the sentence.

A.	captive	capture	captive	
B.	justification	justify	*justifiable *justified	justifiably

*justifiable (done for good reasons and therefore should not be criticized)

*justified (having a good reason for something)

1. It is important for speakers to __capture__ the attention of the audience. A __captive__ audience may not be able to leave the room, but they can go to sleep.

2. In my opinion, there's no __justification__ for not listening to people even though their ideas are different from yours.

Collocations (page 165)

Here are a few polysemous words in this unit. You might ask the class if they know of more than one meaning for these words. If not, they could use their dictionaries to find the meaning of the words in the sentences.

1. *appreciate* (Chapter 17, ¶7)

    a. I appreciate what you have done for me. (*value, esteem highly*)

    b. I'm sure the value of my house will appreciate. (*increase in value*)

2. *lot* (Chapter 19, ¶30)

    a. We played baseball in an open lot. (*empty area, space*)

    b. Many people are not satisfied with their lot in life. (*situation*)

3. *nature* (Chapter 17, ¶1)

    a. I learned to love nature from my parents. (*the natural world not controlled by humans*)

    b. Computers have changed the nature of work. (*character*)

4. *reflect on* (Chapter 17, ¶8)

    a. I hope you will reflect on your decision and perhaps change your mind. (*think about*)

    b. How will your decision reflect on you? (*show you to be*)

5. *take an exam* (Chapter 17, ¶4)

    The students took the exam on Friday. (*ambiguous: wrote the exam/stole/picked up the exam*)

Recommended Readings and Websites

Magnussen, Jemilah. "The Alarming Facts about Factory Farms." *All Animals*, Humane Society of the United States: Summer 2005.

The following websites deal with current topics that raise ethical questions.

http://www1.umn.edu/umnnews/Feature_Stories/The_dope_on_steroids_Why_some_athletes_take_the_risk.html, for ideas concerning why athletes use steroids.

http://www.studentaffairs.cmu.edu/acad_int/why.html, for ideas on why university students cheat.

http://www.buzzle.com/articles/ethical-issues-of-cloning.html, for questions related to the ethics of cloning.

http://www.balancedpolitics.org/assisted_suicide.htm, for the pros and cons of assisted suicide.

www.farmanimalwelfare.org, for information on factory farming.

http://www.bestfoodnation.com/meat-processing.asp, for information on America's meat industry from the industry point of view.

http://medicalmarijuana.procon.org/viewresource.asp?resourceID=000141, for the pros and cons of medical use of marijuana.

UNIT 6: THE ENVIRONMENT

Unit Opener (page 167)

As students discuss the questions and quotes, you can write words related to the unit topic on the board, either those that students use correctly in the discussion or those that they need to learn. After the discussion, have students pronounce any new words and check to see that their meaning is clear. Offer definitions and example sentences as needed. You might improve the discussion by helping students with the vocabulary of the quotes.

The first quote provides an answer to the first question. After students read the second quote and get help with vocabulary, ask how they think it relates to the first quote and how it might relate to the second question. *(Possibly that humans are beginning to see themselves as a single, yet culturally diverse community; possibly that certain cultural groups are overly materialistic and destroying the natural world we all depend on for survival.)*

Mention the existence of the glossary beginning on page 201 of the *Student Book* to help with technical words in this unit.

CHAPTER 21
Humans and Sustainability: An Overview

Before You Read

Previewing (page 168)

This preview is designed to give students realistic objectives for reading the two parts of this long textbook selection; it will also help them read other introductory chapters in the future. Point out the words in boldfaced green and tell students that textbooks often use special text treatments for vocabulary words or new concepts that are defined in the text.

Read (page 169)

Recycling Vocabulary

If students used *World of Reading 2*, ask them if they remember the following vocabulary items: *call for, capacity, concerned, conflict, conventional, expert, facilities, generation, innovative, integrate into, invest, lead to, logical, major, pioneer, satisfied, trade-off, transform,* and *witness*. Select words appropriate for your students, and call on volunteers to explain the meanings or provide them, if necessary. Tell students they will see these items in the reading, but perhaps with new meanings.

Refer to pages 7–8 for ideas on how to review these words in meaningful activities.

LOCATION IN CHAPTER 21	LOCATION IN EARLIER CHAPTERS
appreciate (¶16)	*appreciate:* "Your teacher would not appreciate your viewing the exam ahead of time" (Chapter 17, ¶17)
assessment (subhead Part 2)	*assessed:* "one group of people repeatedly assessed the severity of a continuing personal problem" (Chapter 10, ¶10) "The researchers also assessed the activity of an enzyme called telomerase" (Chapter 11, ¶6)
current (¶11, 22, 29)	*currently:* "Walking produces some other interesting psychological effects, according to studies currently under way" (Chapter 10, ¶12) "They (chimps) are currently being used in research on the nature of hepatitis non-A non-B" (Chapter 19, ¶5)
deal with (subhead Part 1)	*deal with:* "When stress does occur, it is important to recognize and deal with it." (Chapter 9, ¶7)
demands (¶17)	*demand:* "stress . . . a 'non-specific response of the body to a demand.'" (Chapter 9, ¶4)
depleting (¶11–14), *deplete* (¶13)	*depletes:* "the body depletes its resources for fighting stress." (Chapter 9, ¶5)
nature (¶2, 7, 25, 27)	*nature:* "theories about the nature of right and wrong," (Chapter 17, ¶1) "research on the nature of hepatitis non-A non-B" (Chapter 19, ¶5)
outgrowing (¶17)	*outgrown:* "between a young girl who insists that women have outgrown the jumping-on-a-chair-at-the-sight-of-a-mouse era" (Chapter 12, ¶2)
promote (¶9)	*promotes:* "knowing that someone evaluates us positively promotes our attraction to that person." (Chapter 3, ¶4) *promote:* "Congress shall have the power to . . . promote the progress of science" (Chapter 18, ¶4)
rate (n.) (¶7)	*rate:* "I had a group of college students sit for a few minutes and rate their feelings" (Chapter 10, ¶4) "powerful hormones that regulate heart rate" (Chapter 11, Part 2, ¶4)
released (¶18)	*release:* "release the pressure through exercise or physical activity." (Chapter 9, ¶8) "nerve endings that can stimulate the release of catecholamines" (Chapter 11, Part 1, ¶8)
resources (¶1, 4, 7, 11, 15)	*resources:* "the body depletes its resources for fighting stress." (Chapter 9, ¶5) "difficult to commit the kind of resources it takes to discover and develop new talent." (Chapter 18, ¶12)

(continued)

Chapter-by-Chapter Teaching Tips

LOCATION IN CHAPTER 21	LOCATION IN EARLIER CHAPTERS
restore (¶22)	*restore:* "rationalized it as being necessary to restore peace and quiet to the neighborhood." (Chapter 15, ¶6)
shift (n.) (¶22)	*shift:* "to ensure that the mood shift was not due simply to a stroll through the attractive campus surroundings." (Chapter 19, ¶5) "Now, as she (Elaine) settled onto the stool for her shift" (Chapter 20, ¶2)
stabilize (¶22)	*stabilizing:* "Then after stabilizing the patient, it's a matter of waiting it out." (Chapter 11, Part 2, ¶11)
strategies (¶19)	*strategy:* "The best strategy for avoiding stress is to learn how to relax." (Chapter 9, ¶19)
sustainability (title, ¶1), also *sustain, sustainable, sustainably, unsustainability, unsustainably*	*sustain:* "They provide little—if anything—more than the warmth, food and water, and veterinary care required to sustain life." (Chapter 19, ¶24)
wisdom (¶27)	*wise:* "our words of advice are accepted as wise, not intrusive" (Chapter 1, ¶8) *wisdom:* "Folk wisdom tells us that birds of a feather flock together."(Chapter 3, ¶4)

Students may be confused by the meaning of *indefinitely* (MMC) if they think it is a negative of *definitely*. You may help them with the meaning of this word if you discuss what it means to "define a word," or, to give the limits of its meanings. *Indefinitely* means "without limits, forever."

You may want to ask students if they know what a *witness* (MMC) is. Knowing the noun meaning should help them remember the verb meaning.

Vocabulary

Vocabulary Building *(page 176)*

Items 1 and 6, *degrade*: The prefix *de-* from Latin means "down, away, reverse" which should help students remember the meaning of this word. The same prefix appears in *deplete*, but students don't get help from the *-plete* part. Interestingly, *-plete* comes from the Latin word "to fill," so *depleting* is "un + filling" or "emptying." Contrast with *complete*—com (with) + full.

Item 4, *compromise*: Students who see the word *promise* in this word are correct. In the 15th century the word meant to promise with another person to accept an arbiter's decision. In modern English it means to make an agreement in which all parties accept less than they originally wanted. Beware that this word is a false cognate for Spanish speakers; a *compromiso* is a commitment.

Word Analysis *(page 177)*

In this chapter there are two additional words for analysis that use English prefixes. *outgrow* (¶17): *out-* (going beyond) + *grow* = grow too big for something, and *overstate* (¶21): *over-* (too much, in excess) + *state* = exaggerate.

Vocabulary Reminder List

Part 1:

Phrasal verbs: *deal with* [T-not separable] *(first subhead)* = handle; *keep/kept up* [T] (¶1) = continue(d); *live off* (¶11) = get money or food from something in order to live

Collocations: *find a way to* (¶10), *meet the* (current and future) *needs of* (¶11), *in a just and equitable manner* (¶11); *will be gone* (¶12) = will be used up, none will be left

Compound adjectives: *long-term* sustainability (¶1)

Verb/Adjective + preposition: *lead to* (¶1, 8), *interact with* (¶2), *adapt to* (¶3), *transform* (something) *into* (something else) (¶6)

Part 2:

Phrasal verbs: *clean up* [T] (¶15) = clean with idea of completeness added; *call for* [T-not separable] (¶16, 27) = ask publicly that something be done

Collocations: *cite evidence* (¶16), *sustain life on earth* (¶18), *strategies for doing this* (¶19), *the answer to the question of whether* (¶20), *getting better or worse* (¶20), (overstate a problem) *to the point where* (¶21), (make) *an all-out effort to* (¶22), *widely differing views* (¶24), *logically consistent* (¶24), *arrive at* (different) *conclusions* (¶24), *meet* (our) *needs* (¶25), *for* (our) *benefit* (¶25)

Compound adjectives: *life-support* systems (¶16, 19, 25), *energy-based* economy (¶22), *earth-sustaining* and *earth-degrading* forms of economic development (¶27)

Verb/Adjective + preposition: *get trapped into* (¶21), *tend to* (¶21), *lead to* (¶21), *depend on* (¶22, 27), *concerned with* (¶23), *dependent on* (¶27), *integrate into* (¶27), *result in* (¶28)

CHAPTER 22
Islands of Green

Read *(page 181)*

Recycling Vocabulary

If students used *World of Reading 2*, ask them if they remember the following vocabulary items: *actually, contrary to, equivalent, facilities, model* (adj.), *pioneer, public, surface, target, transform,* and *urban*. Select words appropriate for your students, and call on volunteers to explain the meanings or provide them, if necessary. Tell students they will see these items in the reading, but perhaps with new meanings.

Refer to pages 7–8 for ideas on how to review these words in meaningful activities.

LOCATION IN CHAPTER 22	LOCATION IN EARLIER CHAPTERS
heritage (¶4)	*heritage:* "The biological heritage was American, but the cultural training had been Chinese." (Chapter 13, ¶5)
inhabitants (¶4)	*inhabitant:* "he (Winthrop) had seen everything and knew all about the inhabitants" (Chapter 16, ¶25)
inspired (¶5)	*inspired:* "Inspired by our parents' sacrifice, we studied hard to earn scholarships" (Chapter 5, ¶19)
massive (¶5)	*massive:* "These patients came in with what looked like massive heart attacks" (Chapter 11, Part 2, ¶5)
promote (¶7), *promoting* (¶8)	*promoting:* "The cost of recording and promoting a major album can easily top $1 million" (Chapter 18, ¶10) *promote:* "we can promote the planting of tree plantations in areas that have already been cleared or degraded." (Chapter 21, ¶9)
released (¶2)	*releasing:* "His body may respond in the alarm stage by releasing hormones into the bloodstream" (Chapter 9, ¶5) *released:* "In 2005, the *UN's Millennium Ecosystem Assessment* was released." (Chapter 21, ¶18)
resources (¶8)	*resources:* "exponential increases in both the human population and our resource consumption have degraded the air, water, soil," (Chapter 21, ¶1) "natural capital—the natural resources and services that keep us and other species alive" (Chapter 21, ¶4)
restricting (¶5)	*restricting:* "Many of the scientists believe that a bleak, sterile and restricting environment is necessary for their research." (Chapter 19, ¶31)
rush hour (¶5)	*rush-hour:* "Let's take the example of a typical commuter in rush-hour traffic." (Chapter 9, ¶5)
shame (¶4)	*shame:* "as I watched my mother read to him I would feel a surge of resentment and shame." (Chapter 6, ¶3) *ashamed:* "Then maybe you won't be so ashamed of me." (Chapter 6, ¶15)

You might want to check that students understand the referent of *it* in ¶2: "Actually it's something that attracts people . . ." *(the effort to lower emission, lowering emissions)*.

Vocabulary

Vocabulary Building *(page 185)*

Item 6, *porous*: It might help students remember the meaning of this word if they know that the word *pores* refers to the tiny holes in our skin.

Vocabulary Reminder List

Phrasal verbs: *drawing on* [T-not separable] (¶4) = using something to help

Collocations: *look at something the (wrong/right) way* (¶2), *almost four times as many/much as* (¶4), *lead a massive effort to* (¶5), *inspired by* (¶6), *rich in* (¶6), *has done more than any other (someone/something) to* (¶7), *the closest thing to a* (¶7), *leads the way with/in* (¶7), *home of the* (¶8)

Compound adjectives: *car-dependent* sprawl (¶3), *tree-lined* sieve (¶3), *car-free* shopping district (¶7), *British-based* project (¶8), *large-scale* residential development (¶8)

Word Analysis:

infrastructure (¶5): infra (Latin prefix meaning "below, under") + structure = all the systems that support an operation; for example, a city's infrastructure consists of roads, electricity, water, etc.

runoff (¶3): a noun from the verb + prepositional phrase in this sentence: When it rains, water *runs off* the land and into rivers and streams.

CHAPTER 23
Part 1: Think You Can Be a Meat-Eating Environmentalist? Think Again! / Part 2: It's a Plastic World

Read *(page 188)*

Recycling Vocabulary

If students used *World of Reading 2*, ask them if they remember the following vocabulary items: (Part 1) *contribute, determined, scale,* and *sensitive;* (Part 2) *cut down on, focus, miracle, quit, target,* and *ton.* Select words appropriate for your students, and call on volunteers to explain the meanings or provide them, if necessary. Tell students they will see these items in the reading, but perhaps with new meanings.

Refer to pages 7–8 for ideas on how to review these words in meaningful activities.

Part 1:

LOCATION IN CHAPTER 23	LOCATION IN EARLIER CHAPTERS
emissions (¶1)	*emissions:* "reducing carbon emissions to below 1990 levels by 2012" (Chapter 22, ¶22)
massive (¶6)	*massive:* "Peñalosa led a massive effort to transform Bogotá's infrastructure" (Chapter 22, ¶5)
practically (¶8)	*practically:* "Practically all the way back to Mexico, Mr. Winthrop had a notebook in his left hand" (Chapter 16, ¶45)
	"Practically the whole village is related to me (the Indian) somehow or other." (Chapter 16, ¶84)
release (¶6)	*releasing:* "His body may respond in the alarm stage by releasing hormones into the bloodstream" (Chapter 9, ¶5)
	released: "According to data released in June" (Chapter 22, ¶2)

Chapter-by-Chapter Teaching Tips

Part 2:

LOCATION IN CHAPTER 23	LOCATION IN EARLIER CHAPTERS
alert (n.) (¶4, last bullet)	*alert:* "He . . . needed his favorite sweet to stay alert." (Chapter 10, ¶1)
alternative (n.) (¶5)	*alternative:* "And this alternative looks poor when seen from the standpoints of the other students and the teacher." (Chapter 17, ¶9)
biodegradable (¶2, 3); *biodegrade* (¶4, fourth bullet)	*degrade:* "that many human activities degrade natural capital" (Chapter 21, ¶7)
current (¶5)	*currently:* "1,300 chimpanzees . . . currently live in biomedical research labs in the United States" (Chapter 19, update line 6)
	current: "Sustaining our current global civilization now depends on . . ." (Chapter 21, ¶22)
durability (¶6, first bullet)	*durability:* "Sustainability, or durability, is the ability of Earth's various systems . . . to survive and adapt . . . indefinitely." (Chapter 21, ¶3)
estimated (¶4, second bullet)	*estimate:* "the researchers estimate that cells from the highly stressed women resembled cells of low-stressed volunteers who were 10 years older" (Chapter 11, Part 1, ¶7)
institutions (¶7, Step 3)	*institutions:* "how humans and their institutions interact with the natural world" (Chapter 21, ¶2)
resources (¶5)	*resources:* "use only their fair share of Earth's resources" (Chapter 22, ¶8)
toxic (¶2, ¶4, fourth bullet)	*toxic:* "The new findings also suggest that excess catecholamines have a toxic effect on heart tissue" (Chapter 11, Part 2, ¶9)

The instructions in the *Student Book* ask students to preview both readings and choose one. If your class uses this option, you may want to have students do the Comprehension Checks with a classmate who read the same part and then share what they learned with classmates who read the other part. You can also have students read one part in class and the other for homework, or have students read both parts and discuss them as a class.

If all students do not read the article on plastics, you may want to modify the unit test to eliminate *biodegradable, cut down on,* and *wind up* from the cloze exercise and *dispose* from the Word Families.

Vocabulary

Vocabulary Building *(page 193)*

Part 1:

Item 4, *livestock*: If students see the adjective *live* (living) in this word, it should help them remember the meaning.

Part 2:

Item 1, *drawback*: If students remember that *draw* can mean "pull," they may remember that a *drawback* is something negative, something we might pull back from.

Item 3, *disposable*: You may want to relate this word to *dispose of* which means "to throw away" or "get rid of something." Some students might be familiar with the *garbage disposal* system in some kitchen sinks.

Item 8, *viable*: Students might remember this word more easily if they know that *vie* is the French word for "life" (in Latin: *vita*) so the word means "capable of life." (also with this root: *vital, vitamin*)

Item 9, *durability*: If your students read "A Plea for the Chimps," they have seen the words *endure* and *endurance*, which also have the Latin root *dur* which means "to last."

Item 10, *target*: You may want to ask students if they know what a *target* is; knowing the noun meaning should help them remember the verb meaning.

Vocabulary Reminder List

Part 1:

Collocations: *that's the single most important thing you can do* (first quote), *more (something) than all the (multiple things) combined* (¶1, 2), *per day* (¶4), *a reduced risk of* (¶8), *there's no excuse for* (¶8)

Compound adjectives: *meat-eating* environmentalist (title), [also the noun *meat-eater* in (¶3)], *greenhouse-gas* emissions (¶1), *non-native* fish (¶6), *great-tasting, protein-packed* vegetarian foods (¶8)

Verb/Adjective + preposition: *responsible for* (¶1), *account for* (¶3)

Word analysis: *emissions* (¶1): e- (prefix meaning out) + miss (Latin root meaning send) = that which is sent out; related verb: *emit*

Part 2:

Phrasal verbs: *throw away* (T) (subhead, ¶2) = throw into the garbage, dispose of; *move on* (I) (¶6, first bullet) = continue, move to the next matter

Collocations: *take a look around* (your home) (¶1), *on top of that* (¶2), *viable alternative* (¶5), *one way to get the word out* (Step 2)

Verb/Adjective + preposition: *made from* (¶2), *interfere with* (last bullet)

Word analysis: *nanoparticle* (¶4, fourth bullet): nano- comes from Greek and means "dwarf." A nanometer is one billionth of a meter; nanoparticles are extremely small, man-made particles used in various industries.

When discussing Step 4 on page 191 of the *Student Book*, you might want to use the word *landfill* to show English in the process of change. Longman dictionaries give only a noun meaning for this word *(place where waste is buried in large amounts)*. Some people, at least the writers of this book, are starting to use it as a verb meaning "to put in a landfill": "When they're landfilled, they give off methane, a powerful greenhouse gas." (¶7, step 4)

CHAPTER 24
Prayer for the Great Family

Read *(page 196)*

This poem lends itself well to being read aloud. Talk with students about how they could prepare a final reading of the poem. Some ideas include:

- have individuals read the poem with their interpretation of how the prayer should sound
- have an individual read the poem with the whole class coming in on the final line of each stanza
- have each group prepare an individual stanza, with the class joining in on the final line of each stanza

Unit Wrap-Up

Word Families *(page 198)*

The following words in the Word Families in Unit 6 show a shift in primary stress. Draw students' attention to them.

compenSAtion	COMpensate	comPENsatory
MIRacle	miRAculous (-ly)	
sustainaBIlity	susTAIN	(un-) susTAINable (-ly)

Note the difference in the pronunciation of the vowel in the noun *gratitude* [æ] and the adjective *grateful* [eɪ] (line 5 in the chart). There is also a shift in the vowel pronunciation from the adjective *wise* [aɪ] and the noun *wisdom* [ɪ] (line 9 in the chart).

The participial adjective *diversified* (item 3; from the verb *diversify*) suggests that something has been planned or made to be *diverse* (to have many different elements). One common collocation is *diversified investments* in the field of economics. The adjective *diverse* (meaning "very different from each other" or "having very different elements") collocates quite broadly; for example: diverse methods, cultures, products, roles, themes, groups, and perceptions. In this unit, the phrase *diverse mature forests* can be defined as forests with a variety of kinds of trees.

Polysemous Words *(page 199)*

If you want to expand this exercise to include dictionary work, have students look up the meanings for *compromise, ultimate,* and *mock* in the sentences below.

1. *compromise*

   a. By not repairing the machinery, the company <u>compromised</u> employee safety. (*harmed, damaged, risked*)

   b. We disagreed about what to do for a long time, but eventually we <u>compromised</u>. (*agreed, accepted less than we wanted*)

2. *ultimate*

    a. The <u>ultimate</u> responsibility lies with the president of the company. (*final*)

    b. Her <u>ultimate</u> professional objective is to have her own company. (*what happens in the end, eventual*)

    c. These clothes are the <u>ultimate</u> in fashion. (*the best, latest*)

3. *mock*

    a. The comedian <u>mocks</u> politicians in both parties; no one escapes. (*makes fun of*)

    b. Before she applied for the job, Susana did several <u>mock</u> interviews with her friends in order to prepare. (*not real, but like the real thing*)

    c. We have to build a <u>mock-up</u> of our new technology. (*model*)

Linking Readings

Once you complete Unit 6, you might want to have a class or group discussion on the following topics: 1. Relate the three readings in Chapters 22 and 23 to Chapter 21. How do these readings illustrate the concept of sustainability? 2. Reread the definition of environmental science in ¶2 on page 169. Think about how social sciences like economics, politics, and ethics come into play in the three readings in Chapters 22 and 23. What makes these three readings good illustrations of what environmental science is?

Recommended Readings and Websites

Living Unsustainably

Friedman, Thomas. "The Inflection is Near?" *The New York Times*, March 8, 2009.

    Friedman sees 2008 as the beginning of the "Great Disruption," the time "when both Mother Nature and Father Greed have hit the wall at once."

The Greenhouse Effect and Global Warming

McKibben, Bill. "Carbon's New Math." *National Geographic*, October 2007.

    Contains an interesting and brief section on the facts of air pollution.

Krupp, Fred. "U.S. Must Lead by Example." and Kovacs, William L. "Global Treaty a Fool's Paradise." Edited by Steve St. Angelo. *U.S. News and World Report*, April 2009.

    Opposing opinions on the value of international treaties like Kyoto in achieving emissions goals. The whole issue is dedicated to the question of whether Americans can prosper in the new green economy.

"Public Transportation Reduces Greenhouse Gases and Conserves Energy." From The American Public Transportation Association (APTA), available for downloading in PDF format at: http://www.apta.com/research/info/online/greenhouse_brochure.cfm.

    Contains numerous graphs.

Russell, Cristine. "First Wave." *Science News*, February 28, 2009.

    Deals with the effects of rising sea levels on the island nations of The Maldives and Kiribati and their people who may become "climate refugees."

Alternate energy

Clynes, Tom. "The Energy Fix: 10 Steps to End America's Fossil-Fuel Addiction." *Popular Science*, July 2006: 47–61.

> Describes ten technologies for generating renewable energy, including the power of waves and tides.

Feeding Humanity in the Future

Ayres, Ed. "Will We Always Eat Meat?" *All Animals*, Summer 2000.

Jacobson, Michael. "Diet for a Cooler Planet." *Nutrition Action Healthletter*, May 2007.

> These articles discuss both the need for and benefit of eating more plants and less meat.

http://www.verticalfarm.com/, for a look at the future of food grown in buildings in the center of cities.

Biodiversity

Wilson, Edward O. "Unmined Riches." In *The Diversity of Life*. Cambridge: Belknap Press, 1992.

> Shows how protecting ecosystems, especially forests, can provide sustainable economic growth for countries, making it more profitable to conserve resources than to destroy them.

Student Book Answer Key

Since previewing is less structured in World of Reading 3, *answers are more likely than usual to vary. The answers suggested in this answer key are minimal; your students may come up with fuller answers, depending on how they preview.*

UNIT 1: FRIENDSHIP

CHAPTER 1
All Kinds of Friends

Before You Read

Previewing, *page 2*
1. convenience, special-interest, cross-generational, close friends
2. *Answers will vary.*

Read, *pages 3–4*

a, b, a, a, b, b

Comprehension Check

First Reading, *page 4*
1. informal discussions with people (¶2), not scientific research
2. friends are important to each other, they make our lives better, they accept us as we are, having friends heightens our self-esteem (¶1)
3. convenience friends, special-interest friends

Second Reading, *pages 4–5*
1. Special-interest friends: "depend on sharing some activity or concern," "participate jointly," "*doing* together, not *being* together"

   Paraphrase: Special-interest friends share a cause they are involved in together or a sport that they play together, but they aren't close friends.

   Cross-generational friends: "unequal," "form across generations," "daughter-mother and mother-daughter relationships"

   Paraphrase: Cross-generational friendships are friendships between older and younger people.

   Close friends: "ongoing friendships of deep intimacy," "involve revealing aspects of our private self," "involve important rights and obligations"

   Paraphrase: Close friends are intimate friends who reveal a lot to each other and do a lot for each other.

2. b. D "regularly involved without being intimate"
   c. A "because we are unconnected by blood, our words of advice are accepted as wise, not intrusive"
   d. D "we may not expose as much—or the same kinds of things—to each of our closest friends"
   e. A "frequently turn . . . not to our blood relations but to friends"

3. b
   a. not accurate, contradicts Viorst's main idea
   c. too narrow
   d. contains an addition
   e. too general

Vocabulary

Vocabulary Building, *page 6*

1. e	5. a	9. c
2. j	6. g*	10. h*
3. i	7. f	
4. b	8. d	

*Students might argue that letter 'h' is the correct answer for #6; however, it is needed for #10.

Word Analysis, *page 7*
2. en/rich: *en-* means *make*; *enrich* means *make rich, make better*
3. silver/ware: *silver* is a type of metal; *-ware* means things made of a particular material; *silverware* refers to knives, spoons, forks (originally made of silver)
4. over/weight: *over-* means in excess, too much; *overweight* means weighing too much, having excess weight, too heavy
5. un/equal: *un-* means not, *equal* means the same; *unequal* means not the same, not equal

68 World of Reading 3 *Teacher's Manual*

6. en/liv/en: *en* both as a prefix and a suffix means *make*; *enliven* means make something more lively, give it life
7. on/going: (related to phrasal verb *go on*) going on, continuing
8. re/assur/ance: the base *assure* means to make someone feel more sure (secure), *re-* is an intensifying prefix, *-ance* is a noun-making suffix; *reassurance* is something that makes you feel less worried or unsure (such as support, comfort)

Vocabulary Review, *page 7*
1. mentor, intrusive
2. intersect
3. obligation, reassurance
4. enhance, broaden
5. intimate

Text Analysis

Lists, *page 8*

from less intimate to more intimate friendships

Making Definitions Clearer with Specific Examples, *page 8*

Convenience Friends: may be part of the same car pool, lend each other things, drive each other's kids to their activities when the other is sick, take care of a pet when one goes on vacation, give each other lifts to pick up the car at the mechanic

Special-interest Friends: play a sport together, work in the same place, take yoga class together, or are involved in a cause together

CHAPTER 2
Online Friendships

Before You Read

Previewing, *page 9*
1. The author's attitude will probably be mixed. The section which has the heading that includes the words, "It can be good for you!" is the longest; however, there are headings that indicate something negative: "When to Be Careful" and "Caught in the Net? Keeping Yourself Safe Online." Also, the first sentences of ¶10 and ¶18 allude to negative aspects.
2. very common (¶1)

Read, *pages 9–11*

b, b, a, b, a, b, a

Comprehension Check

First Reading, *page 12*
1. students/teenagers and adult experts; The teens provide examples from personal experience. The adults provide research findings and analyses of the needs and behavior of teens; they also warn of some dangers of socializing online. The box gives advice from an adult expert on how to be careful.
2. a

Second Reading, *page 12*
1. Marcus likes online role-playing games, but he likes it better when some of his real-world friends are also playing (¶3).
2. Lauren B. goes to a big high school, so she IM's friends after school because she doesn't see them during the day (¶4).
3. Mike lives in the U.S. now and keeps in touch with both local friends and friends from the school he went to in England (¶6).
4. When Lauren J. moved from Texas to Maryland, she was able to keep in touch with her old friends in Texas. Now she's moving back and doesn't feel out of touch because she was able to keep up with her old friends while she was away. Now she has friends in Maryland to keep in touch with, too (¶9).
5. All of these students are keeping in touch with real-world friends.
6. Teens need to feel connected, and experts think IM is a good tool for keeping in touch with core friends while establishing relationships that are not as close; teens need both (¶8). Aftab thinks it's easier for teens to be themselves online because they are judged by their ideas, not by their appearance or their possessions. Aftab and Hersch both think it is a way of enlarging your circle of friends and finding people who share your interests or with whom you have something in common. Hersch believes it's a good place to explore feelings and communicate at a deeper level and more honestly (¶12–14).
7. Negative aspects include gossip and fights that begin face-to-face which are carried on online and can seem meaner than intended (¶10, 11). There are dangers: People can pretend they are someone else. There can be bullying and fighting. The box lists ways to be careful: Don't give personal information, especially to people you don't know face-to-face, watch out for adults posing as teens, and have a friend (a

"cyberbuddy") who tells you what not to put on your social networking page. Also, be willing to back out of a questionable situation (¶17).
8. It will be much easier to keep in touch long-term with people, even after they move on in life (go to college, etc.).

Vocabulary

Vocabulary Building, page 13

1. d	5. i	9. k
2. f	6. j	10. b
3. e	7. h	11. g
4. a	8. c	

Multiword Expressions, pages 13–14

1. just as (good) as
2. keep in touch with
3. a (pretty) big deal
4. keeping up with
5. hang out with
6. kept up
7. break up with
8. beat up
9. back out of
10. taking over
11. a lifetime's worth of
12. look over

Vocabulary Review, page 14

1. enlarging, bulk, keep in touch
2. core
3. taking over, hanging out
4. cautious, posing
5. forever

Text Analysis, page 15

Although Jan Farrington, the author, makes general statements and frames information from teens and experts, either the teen or the expert is the focus.

¶6: question posed by author, answer given by teen (Mike L.)
¶7–8: researchers and experts
¶9: teen (Lauren J.)
¶10–11: teen (Lauren B.)
¶12: expert (Patricia Hersch)
¶13–14: expert (Parry Aftab)
¶15: expert (Parry Aftab) and teen (Lauren J.)
¶16: teen (Lauren J.)
¶17: author (Jan Farrington)
¶18–19: author
box: expert (Parry Aftab)

Chapter 3
How Do I Like Thee? Let Me Count the Ways

Before You Read

Previewing, page 16

1. b
2. a
3. a
4. b
5. b
6. characteristics or qualities of friends

Read, page 17

a, b, a, b, a, b

Comprehension Check

First Reading, page 18

1. proximity, exposure, similarity, reciprocity-of-liking, and physical attractiveness
2. keeping confidences, loyalty, warmth and affection (followed closely by supportiveness, frankness, sense of humor)

Second Reading, page 18

1. T (¶2)	4. T (¶5)
2. F (¶3)	5. F (¶5)
3. T (¶4)	6. F (graph)

Vocabulary

Vocabulary Building, page 19

1. b	5. f	9. h
2. e	6. d	10. a
3. i	7. j	
4. c	8. g	

Vocabulary Review, pages 19–20

1. critical
2. proximity
3. exposure
4. traits
5. reciprocity
6. contradicts, attractive
7. promote

Text Analysis, *pages 20–21*

1. Bates: journal article
   Burgoon et al.: journal article
   Festinger et al.: book
   Harvey & Weber: book
   Kruglanski et al.: journal article
   Metee & Aronson: chapter in a book
   Parlee: magazine article
   Zajonc: journal article

2. b, c, a, d

CHAPTER 4
The First Day of School

Before You Read

Previewing, *page 22*

1. Jim, Dr. Davy (Jim's father), Jim's mother (deceased), and Amy (the housekeeper)
2. Jim and Amy
3. The story will probably describe Jim's first day of school.

Read, *pages 22–25*

a, a, b, b, b, a, b, a

Comprehension Check, *page 25*

1. Jim's mother died when he was born. Jim is an only child. His father is a doctor, French, 40 years old; the father came from a poor, unhappy, yet ambitious family.
2. Jim likes Amy (lines 7, 91–93); she's like a mother to him, but he's blaming her for making him start school.
3. He's not happy about starting school. We know by the way he talks to Amy (lines 11, 16–18, 23–24, etc.).
4. Amy, who never went to school herself, understands his fear but knows he has to go to school. She's frightened by the building, does not like the principal, Mr. Barber, and worries about Jim when she leaves him there the first day.
5. Jim makes friends with other children by breaking the teacher's rule about not chewing gum, and also by exchanging jokes and being funny.
6. Dr. Davy starts to pay more attention to Jim at the end of the story. Amy is delighted.
7. They all change. Jim was probably a lonely only child before he met other children in school; he becomes social and playful. Dr. Davy was probably the type of father who doesn't really know how to relate to very young children. At the end of the story he changes as he sees his son become a more interesting person. Amy changes from being afraid about starting Jim in school and being unhappy about Dr. Davy's lack of a relationship with his son. She becomes happy to see Jim likes at least the social aspects of school. She is also very happy to see Dr. Davy take an interest in Jim.

Vocabulary

Vocabulary Building: Synonyms, *page 26*

1. a, c   4. b, c   7. b, c
2. b, c   5. a, c   8. b, c
3. b, c   6. a, b

Vocabulary Review, *pages 26–27*

1. scared
2. got along
3. funny
4. on the way
5. delighted

Text Analysis

Chronological Order, *page 27*

b. before line 33 ("The school building was very ugly . . .")
c. before line 55 ("Miss Binney, the teacher of the first grade, . . .")
d. before line 71 ("Amy was in the hall . . .")
e. before line 83 ("In the morning . . .")
f. before line 103 ("Miss Binney said, Jim Davy, . . .")
g. before line 126 ("He told his father . . .")

Point of View, *page 27*

a. the omniscient author; lines 1–5 give information only the author knows, the story is told in the 3rd person
b. *Answers will vary.*

Unit Wrap-Up

Word Families, *page 28*

1. apologetic
2. caution, cautiously
3. contradictory
4. exposure
5. intensified
6. intrude
7. obligatory
8. supportive

Polysemous Words, *pages 29–30*

1. b, a
2. b, b, a
3. c, b, a
4. b, a, a
5. c, d, a, b
6. a, b, a

UNIT 2: PARENTS AND CHILDREN

CHAPTER 5
Mother Was Really Somebody

Before You Read

Previewing, *page 33*

1. very positive, she challenged her children, urged them to "think big," had confidence in them, and expected them to go to college and do well
2. an adult child

Read, *pages 33–36*

a, a, b, a, a, a, b, a, b, b, a, a

Comprehension Check

First Reading, *page 36*

1. Both were immigrants from Italy. Mrs. Michelotti came to the U.S. in 1926 when she was 3 and grew up in Chicago. She was at the top of her high-school class, went to secretarial school, and worked as an executive secretary for a railroad company until she got married. Mr. Michelotti came to the U.S. when he was 17 and sold candy to office workers on their break. He had less education but built a successful wholesale candy business. (*Wholesale* means he sold to retailers who, in turn, sold directly to customers.) Carlo and Anna married in 1944 and in 1950 moved to a farm 40 miles outside of Chicago.
2. Mr. Michelotti was quiet, religious, intelligent, but had little formal schooling. He worked hard and was successful in establishing a small business as well as having a farm. Mrs. Michelotti was more outgoing, people-oriented, and very generous. When she married, she gave up the idea of a career in order to be a traditional homemaker and mother who dedicated her life to her children.
3. Mrs. Michelotti was devoted to her husband, admired his accomplishments, and set him up as an example for the children. It was a traditional marriage in which the father worked and the mother dedicated herself to raising the children and keeping house.
4. harmonious, happy, caring, close, religious, goal-oriented; they were supportive of each other
5. Joseph feels proud of her and all that she did for her children. She was "the driving influence in my decision to become a physician" (¶31). He appreciates the lessons she taught him as he was growing up. He appreciates the love and caring she showed, for example, when his parents came to the hospital in the middle of the night to make sure he was OK.

Second Reading, *page 36*

1. Mrs. Michelotti set Carlo up as an example of a person who accomplished a lot and made it clear to the children that

72 *World of Reading 3 Teacher's Manual*

they too could accomplish a lot; she gave them positive reinforcement for all they did (wobbly bookcase, paint-by-number pictures); she helped them with school work, she praised good report cards, and she let them know that they could do whatever they decided (for example, when Carla was 12 and said she wanted to be a lawyer, her mother encouraged her).
2. She participated in their education by helping them at home and compensating for the limitations of their small rural school—providing educational toys, talking to them about history, politics, and current events. She also helped to arrange a field trip to Chicago and acted as a tour guide. Going to college was simply assumed to be something all of them would do.
3. She said she preferred a letter from a child about him/herself instead of a store-bought birthday gift. The best gift from her children was for them to develop well and to keep communication with her open.
4. She always attended any school activity in which one of her children was involved (a production of *The Music Man*, inauguration as president of the National Honor Society). She also made sure siblings participated in each other's accomplishments because the family was a unit. This extended to recreation and religion (¶24–26).
5. She was generous with the neighbors' children. As her children became professionals, she inspired them to help others (¶28). Her letter to Leo upon receiving his Ph.D. in physics is one such example, and she was the inspiration for Joseph to enter a helping profession.

Vocabulary

Vocabulary Building, *page 37*

Part 1:

1. f
2. a
3. d
4. b
5. c
6. g
7. e

Part 2:

8. k
9. m
10. l
11. h
12. n
13. j
14. i

Using a Dictionary, *page 38*

Definitions are based on Longman's learners' dictionaries of American English (*Longman Dictionary of American English* and *Advanced American Dictionary*).

2. limp: walk with difficulty because one leg is hurt
   stumble: walk in an unsteady way almost falling down
3. was devoted to: gave someone a lot of love, concern, and attention
   devotion: strong feeling of love shown by paying a lot of attention to someone
4. commuted: traveled regularly to get to work
5. spy: suddenly see, spot
   stare: look for a long time without moving your eyes
   gaze (out): look for a long time, especially without realizing you are doing it
6. point out: show by pointing
7. recount: tell a story or describe a series of events (formal)
8. hustle: make someone move quickly, often by pushing them
9. rummage: search for something by moving things around
10. exhausted: extremely tired

Vocabulary Review, *pages 38–39*

1. hectic
2. isolated
3. accomplishments
4. chores
5. nurtured, potential

Text Analysis, *page 39*

1. Introduction: (¶1–3) The article starts with something that happened in the author's adult life, setting readers up for a flashback. ¶3 suggests why he wrote the article—to show how his mother was a mentor, something he didn't fully appreciate until he was an adult (last sentence of ¶3).
2. Body: (¶4–32) He makes statements about his mother and supports them with specific examples.
3. Conclusion: (¶33–36) The conclusion gives facts about the end of Mrs. Michelotti's life and her children's thoughts about their mother, referring back to comments in the body. It also reiterates her pride in her children and adds that the children are the ones who are proud of her. The last clause refers to the title giving unity to the piece of writing.

CHAPTER 6
The Problems of Fathers and Sons

Before You Read

Previewing, *page 41*

1. a child's point of view (though written by the adult child)
2. the fact that his father is illiterate

Read, *pages 41–43*

a, a, b, a, b, a, a, b, a, b, b, b

Comprehension Check

First Reading, *page 43*

1. strengths: he's a great storyteller, good at his job, handy (could fix machinery and electrical appliances), knew a lot (could answer his son's questions); weakness: he was illiterate
2. The wife reads him the newspaper every evening. She has tried to teach him to read and has taught him to copy his name.
3. The owner, Mr. Fenner, refused to accept Mr. López' check with his copied signature even though Mr. López signed the check right in front of him. Hank, the son, gets very mad at his father for being unable to write and at Fenner for not accepting the signature. He throws a can of furniture polish at Fenner and runs out of the store.
4. He felt guilty for yelling at his father (¶13).
5. The mother never succeeds in teaching her husband to read and write.

Second Reading, *page 44*

1. a. He felt resentment and shame.
   b. He felt frustrated and furious.
   c. He was annoyed by his father's use of Spanish. He felt shame and resentment. He was furious with Fenner.
   d. He felt guilty.
2.
   b. U Hank admires many things about his father (strengths mentioned in the First Reading, question 1). However, his frustration could (but didn't) turn to hatred (¶6).
   c. U Hank wants his father to be able to read and write; that does not imply perfection. Some students may find this a reasonable inference if one could assume Hank thought his father was nearly perfect, illiteracy being his only fault.
   d. U He respects the things his father is good at; his strengths. He also knows that yelling at his father was disrespectful.
   e. R Fenner knew who Mr. López was and that he was the one who signed (endorsed) the check. Not accepting the signature was unjustifiably mean.
   f. R He was so angry that he probably did want to hurt Mr. Fenner; he aimed at his head (¶13).
   g. R The father asks his wife to try again to teach him so that the son will not be so ashamed of him (¶15).

Vocabulary

Vocabulary Building—Using Paraphrases, *page 45*

1. articulate = able to express ideas clearly; fascinating = very interesting; illiterate = unable to read or write
2. surge of resentment = increased anger; shame = embarrassment
3. console = make (me) feel better; hero = a person you admire a lot
4. ignorance = not knowing certain things; bear = tolerate
5. humble = lowly and simple; full = complete
6. painstaking = requiring very careful effort
7. glanced = looked quickly; sheepishly = with an embarrassed look; leering = with a look of superiority
8. flung (past of *fling*) myself = threw myself; lawn = grass; wept = cried; exhaustion = extreme tiredness, with no more energy left
9. multisyllabic words = long words (with several syllables); accurately = correctly; beyond his grasp = more than he could understand, not comprehensible

Using a Dictionary, *page 46*

2. stomp: step hard on the ground when walking, usually to show anger
3. stagger: walk in an unsteady way
4. bulbous: fat, round, and unattractive (the shape of a light bulb)
   squinty: partly closed
5. smirk: unkind smile showing pleasure in someone else's bad luck

6. squirm: twist (turn) your body from side to side because you are uncomfortable or nervous
7. grab: take hold of something with a sudden or violent movement
8. twist: turn part of your body around while the rest stays still

Vocabulary Review, *page 47*

1. fascinating
2. illiterate, ignorance
3. humble, painstaking
4. beyond his grasp

Text Analysis, *page 47*

¶1–8 c,   ¶9 d,   ¶10–15 a,   ¶16 b

This selection starts with background information about a problem and the child's feelings about it. It is followed by an anecdote illustrating the boy's emotions and ends with a conclusion or final comment. The parts are problem, illustration, and conclusion. This is not typical IBC; however, one could argue that the exposition of the problem is an introduction, the anecdote is the body, and the final comment is the conclusion.

CHAPTER 7
Greener Grass

Before You Read

Previewing, *page 48*

1. The author is divorced, and the main chore she hasn't been able to do herself is maintain the lawn.
2. José is from Guatemala; he works as a landscaper.
3. The author hires José to take care of her lawn.

Read, *pages 48–50*

a, b, b, b, a

Comprehension Check

First Reading, *page 50*

1. T (¶2)
2. F (¶2, 3)
3. F (¶2, 3)
4. T (¶3, 7)
5. T (¶4, 9)

Second Reading, *pages 50–51*

1. José couldn't support his family in Guatemala (¶2).
2. He came every Tuesday (¶3) and sent other workers when he couldn't come (¶5).
3. Freddy wanted to be called Freddy Krueger, a horror-movie character (¶3). They take jobs in other parts of the U.S., suggesting that they want to move up the economic ladder and become more independent; in other words, make their own way in their new country (¶6).
4. José is sad and lonely; he cries (¶6). He thinks he might go back to Guatemala (¶12).
5. She couldn't believe her daughter wanted to be so far away from her mother, their home, and their life in Southern California (¶4).
6. She has some understanding of José's situation but realizes that their situations are different (¶13).
7. The American dream is to be successful and for children to do better than their parents, which means parents must let go of their children in order for them to move on. **José:** He migrates to the U.S. to make money, but he is upset when his sons do not want to continue working with him and choose to move on. **Henry** and **Freddy:** They want to pursue the American dream and strike out on their own. **The author:** She is not as affected by the American dream as an immigrant. Although she is not happy about her daughter going to college far away, she understands the American dream and has to accept the way her daughter chooses to better herself.

Vocabulary

Vocabulary Building, *page 51*

1. d   4. a   7. e
2. c   5. h   8. g
3. f   6. b

Vocabulary Review, *pages 51–52*

1. hired
2. visas
3. envied
4. convince
5. made up his mind

Text Analysis, page 52

1. The fact that her daughter wanted to go far away to college coupled with the fact that José's sons also chose to move far away.
2. She touches on two issues: 1. The issue of immigration and the separation of immigrant families. 2. The issue of letting children go. She doesn't deal with the first issue in her essay, but she does learn something about it from José. She reluctantly accepts letting her daughter go.
3. Although her own daughter's decision to go to college far away may have inspired Straight to write this essay, she probably wants to share the insight she gained into the family life of separated immigrant families with a wider audience.

CHAPTER 8
Love, Your Only Mother

Read, pages 53–55

b, a, a, a

Comprehension Check, pages 55–56

1. The daughter is the narrator; she is addressing her mother.
2. The mother left her husband and daughter in 1959 when the daughter was 7. The daughter is now an adult. She is married with a daughter of her own.
3. The mother started sending postcards four months after leaving, but the communication is one-way as there is never an adequate return address. In addition, the mother does not seem to be staying in one place.
4. The postcards are sent from small towns mostly in the middle of the U.S.: Enid, Oklahoma; Ferndale, Nebraska (but there is no such place as Ferndale in Nebraska); Sioux City, Iowa; Jackson Falls, Horseshoe Bend, Truckee (California); Elm City, Spivey, Kansas; Manning, North Dakota; Tupelo, Mississippi. Some of these are quite distant from each other.
5. She tells people her mother is in whatever town the last postcard came from. She shows them the place on the map in the atlas.
6. The messages are short and often strange like the one about the beetles (¶5). Once the mother promised to send a birthday cake; once she said she had left something for the daughter in a safety deposit box (¶7). The messages don't make a lot of sense. The odd thing in the signature is the word *only* (¶8, 10). The daughter probably keeps the postcards because that is all she has of her mother. They are the history of their life together, so to speak (¶12, 15).
7. The husband thinks the situation is crazy, and his wife should forget about her mother. But he does comfort her when she has nightmares and is terrified that her mother might come back. He reassures her that she'll never come back.
8. The daughter has probably always felt somehow abnormal, different from her friends. In a way, the messages on the postcards are her mother's voice haunting her "like a buoy in the fog." Like a buoy, the mother's voice guides or influences the daughter's life.
9. *Answers will vary.* One possibility: "Why did the mother leave?"

Vocabulary

Vocabulary Building, page 56

1. h   5. a   9. c
2. j   6. d   10. b
3. f   7. g
4. e   8. i

Vocabulary Review, pages 56–57

1. wandered
2. brief
3. wonders, vowed
4. terrified
5. grunts

Text Analysis, page 57

1. It suggests that the mother was leaving the father; perhaps she feels guilty about having abandoned her daughter as well.
2. the age the daughter was when the mother left (7 years old), the fact that the daughter has graduated from college and has had several apartments, the daughter is now married and has a daughter of her own
3. The husband's attitude is marginally tolerant: he grunts (¶2). He asks, "What craziness is it this time?" (¶6) Yet he comforts his wife when she has nightmares that her mother has returned.
4. The word *distance* occurs in ¶10 and does refer to physical distance, which the

76 *World of Reading 3 Teacher's Manual*

mother suggests means nothing, and the daughter thinks this means the mother might come back or maybe the emotional distance is not great. No matter how far away, she always finds the daughter (¶11). In (¶19) the adult daughter seems to go away—not physical distance—(her daughter asks why she's "standing there like that") but she comes back, maintaining the distance between herself and the mother who never returned. The terror passes only when the husband says she'll never come back—the distance is great and permanent. The repeated references to distance point to the totally disengaged (detached, distant) parent, and the sad effect that had on the daughter—although she has managed to grow up, go to college and become an apparently normal adult.

Unit Wrap-Up

Word Families, *pages 58–59*

1. consolation
2. flattery
3. infuriated, furious
4. frustrated
5. guilty
6. illiterate
7. proudly
8. resented
9. shame
10. terrifying

Polysemous Words, *pages 59–60*

1. d, a, b, d, c
2. b, a, c,
3. d, b, a, c
4. b, a, b
5. a, c, b
6. b, e, d, a, c
7. e, b, d, a, c
8. a, c, b

UNIT 3 STRESS

CHAPTER 9
Plain Talk about Handling Stress

Before You Read

Previewing, *page 63*

1. "Plain talk" is clear, simple, and straightforward. In this case it probably means non-technical, without medical jargon.
2. the general public—all ordinary people
3. He will probably tell readers what (chronic) stress is and what they can do about it.
4. purpose: to inform people and help them improve their lives
   likely to be found in: public health offices, clinics, doctors' offices

Read, *pages 64–66*

a, b, b, a, a, a, b, a

Comprehension Check

First Reading, *page 66*

1. Life would be boring with no stress at all; stress makes life more exciting and challenging.
   Good stress becomes bad (distress) when there is too much stress over long periods of time.
2. c ("a" is incorrect because the article is not principally about acute stress; "b" is too general)
3. There are two acceptable answers: the last sentence in ¶1; the second sentence in ¶6.

Student Book Answer Key **77**

Second Reading, *page 66*

1. The three stages are alarm, resistance, and exhaustion. Alarm involves perspiring and getting red in the face. It may involve anger, fear, frustration, a bad feeling in the stomach, and tension in the arms and legs. Resistance involves repair work to the body. Exhaustion involves depletion of the body's ability to fight stress (¶5).

2.

SUGGESTION	PARAPHRASE	INFERRED CAUSE
Know your limits	Don't fight it if you can't change something, at least for the time being.	You are the type of person who tries to fix all problems.
Take care of yourself	Get enough sleep and eat well.	You are not taking good enough care of your health.
Make time for fun	Everyone needs a break.	You are not taking time for recreation.
Be a participant	Be sociable and keep busy and involved in some type of volunteer work; it can make you feel better.	You are not involved in enough other things.
Check off your tasks	Make a list of what you have to do, putting the most important ones first. Check each one off when you get it done.	You are not organized in the way you deal with tasks.
Must you always be right?	You'll get along better with people and feel less stressed if you are more flexible and cooperative rather than confrontational.	You get upset when other people don't do things they way you think they should.
It's OK to cry	Crying can relieve tension and prevent some of the physical effects of stress such as headaches.	You keep tension and emotional distress bottled up.
Create a quiet scene	Imagining a peaceful scene is an escape from stress. The same thing can be accomplished by reading a good book, playing, or listening to music.	You don't get away from the stressful, hectic situations that cause stress.
Avoid self-medication	Medication provides only temporary relief from stress. It may be habit forming, can impair your efficiency, and create more stress.	You use or are tempted to use medication to relieve stress.

Vocabulary

Vocabulary Building, page 67

Part 1:

1. g
2. f
3. b
4. a
5. c
6. e
7. d

Part 2:

8. k
9. j
10. i
11. l
12. n
13. h
14. m

Multiword Expressions, page 68

1. cope with stress
2. taking it easy
3. rush-hour traffic, traffic jams
4. close calls
5. deal with
6. come up with
7. feeling sorry for
8. on your way to
9. give and take
10. tune out
11. get out of hand

Vocabulary Review, page 68

There are several items where one might argue that there are two possible answers. However, students should pay attention to collocations: *relieve stress/tune out problems.*

1. close call
2. prolonged
3. overwhelmed
4. relieve
5. take it easy, tune out
6. get out of hand, bored

Text Analysis, page 69

A.
1. -ing
2. -ed

B.
1. boring, bored
2. exciting
3. frustrated
4. relaxed, relaxing
5. irritating, irritated

CHAPTER 10
Energy Walks

Before You Read

Previewing, page 71

1. Students could answer either way, but the article will say that physical exercise gives more lasting energy than the candy bar. Evidence is found in the subhead, where the phrase "join me for a brisk walk" in ¶1, all of ¶8, and the first sentence of ¶9, suggests that sugar causes fatigue.
2. b.

Read, pages 71–73

a, a, b, b, b a, b, a

Comprehension Check

First Reading, page 73

1. a brisk or moderately fast walk for 10 minutes (¶1–2)
2. The positive effect of walking lasts longer, doesn't result in fatigue later, is less fattening, and has other positive effects (¶3).
3. increases optimism, reduces tension and blood pressure, makes personal problems seem less serious, can help if you are trying to quit smoking

Second Reading, pages 73–74

1. Robert E. Thayer's; he is a professor at California State University in Long Beach. Mention is also made of James Rippe's research (¶5) and other researchers (¶9).
2. Subjects were young or middle-aged people in reasonably good physical condition (college students).

3.

EXPERIMENT	RESEARCH QUESTIONS	PROCEDURES	FINDINGS
1 (¶4)	What is the effect of a 10-minute brisk walk on energy level and tension?	Rated feelings of energy and tension on a checklist, took a 10-minute walk on campus, and filled out the checklist again within five minutes.	Subjects felt more energetic, less tired after the walk.
2 (¶5)	Was the effect due to the attractive campus surroundings?	Same as experiment 1 except subjects walked on a treadmill in a bare room instead of around campus.	Same as experiment 1.
3A (¶6–7)	How long does the effect last?	Subjects took 10-minute walks over a period of three weeks, rated energy and tension levels before the walk and several times during the two hours following the walk.	There was a significant positive effect 20 minutes after the walk, which lasted at least an hour. Even two hours later there was some increased energy effect.
3B (¶8)	What is the difference in effect of walking and eating a sugar snack?	Same procedure as experiment 3A, but subjects ate a candy bar instead of walking.	The immediate mood change was a similar energy boost, but after an hour subjects started to feel more tired and tense.
4 (¶10–11)	What is the effect of walking on optimism and attitude toward personal problems?	Over a period of three weeks, one group of subjects rated how severe personal problems seemed; another group rated how optimistic they felt. Both groups took the 10-minute walk each time they filled out the rating sheet, which was at fixed times each day.	After walking, personal problems seemed less serious, and optimism increased. The increase in effect got larger by the end of the three weeks.

4. Sugar increases the level of serotonin in the brain. Since serotonin is a sedative, it can cause fatigue (¶9).

Vocabulary

Vocabulary Building, *pages 74–75*

1. b
2. a
3. b
4. b
5. b
6. b
7. c
8. c
9. a
10. c
11. b

Vocabulary Review, *page 76*

1. alert
2. brisk
3. pick-me-up, fatigue
4. tip

Text Analysis, *page 76*

¶3–12: describe various experiments

¶13: summarizes, gives instructions for energy walking, and offers encouragement

The organization is introduction, body, and conclusion.

CHAPTER 11
Part 1: Stressed to Death
Part 2: Heartfelt Fear

Before You Read

Previewing, *page 77*

1. Heartfelt Fear
2. Stressed to Death

Read, *pages 77–80*

Part 1:

a, a, b, a, b, b, b

Part 2:

a, b, b, a, b, a, b, b

Comprehension Check

First Reading, *page 80*

Part 1:

1. One group consisted of 39 mothers who were primary caregivers for a child who was chronically ill; the other 19 mothers had normal, healthy children.
2. the mothers with a sick child; chronic stress
3. The effect of stress on these women accelerated aging of cells.

Part 2:

1. after a traumatic event such as the death of a spouse, a car accident, a robbery, a family argument, having to appear in court, or even a surprise party; acute stress
2. Emergency room physicians should question patients to find out if such an event has taken place because there is no need to treat these patients as if they had a heart attack.
3. All of these patients recovered (¶7).

Second Reading, *pages 80–82*

Part 1:

A. 1. T (¶3)
   2. F (¶3)
   3. T (¶2)
   4. T (¶7)
   5. T (¶8)
   6. T (¶7, 2)
   7. F (¶4, 7) (All the subjects had children; the article does not say anything about women without children.)

B. 1. telomerase
   2. free radicals
   3. shorter telomeres
   4. telomere
   5. divide
   6. die

Part 2:

A. 1. F (¶2, 5)
   2. T (¶2)
   3. T (¶2, 3)
   4. F (¶4)
   5. T (¶8)
   6. T (¶11, 12)
   7. F (¶10)

B.

	STUDY 1	**STUDY 2**
1. Researcher:	Champion	Sharkey
2. Subjects:	18 women, 1 man	22 women (All subjects had heart attack symptoms, but no clogged coronary arteries or damaged tissue.)
3. Technology:	blood samples	MRI
4. Findings:	abnormally high levels of catecholamine hormones	abnormality in wall of ventricle caused impaired pumping, so not enough blood was circulated

Vocabulary

Vocabulary Building, pages 82–83

Part 1:

1. g
2. a
3. e
4. c
5. b
6. i
7. f
8. d
9. h

Part 2:

1. h
2. f
3. b
4. c
5. g
6. d
7. i
8. e
9. a

Finding Definitions in the Text, page 83

Part 1:

1. telomeres: protein-DNA complexes that tell a cell how long to live
2. mononucleocytes: immune cells in the blood
3. telomerase: an enzyme that maintains telomeres

Part 2:

1. catecholamine: hormones, including adrenaline and dopamine, which increase when a person has a heart attack, but apparently increase even more under conditions of acute stress
2. adrenaline and dopamine: hormones that regulate heart rate, blood pressure, and other body processes; they are catecholamines

Vocabulary Review, page 84

Part 1:

1. resembled
2. striking
3. speculate, impede
4. underpinnings, haggard

Part 2:

1. symptoms, triggered
2. clogged, abnormal
3. impaired, circulated
4. recovered

Text Analysis, page 85

1. no
2. in journals mentioned in the article
3. The authors quote the researchers and other scientists.
4. no
5. the institutional affiliation of the person quoted
6. Scholars are likely to want to read the original work and need to be able to find it. They may also evaluate the source.

CHAPTER 12
The Dinner Party

Read, pages 86–87

b, a, b, b, a

82 World of Reading 3 Teacher's Manual

Comprehension Check, *page 87*

1. The question was whether women still reacted with helpless fear at things like the sight of a mouse. A young woman at the dinner party claimed that women had outgrown such behavior while a colonel disagreed and claimed that men had more control.
2. He notices the hostess' expression and that she calls a servant; when the servant brings a bowl of milk, he knows that it is bait for a snake.
3. It is clever of him to make a bet that will keep the guests quiet until the snake is safely out of the room. His solution turns out to be doubly clever since it also serves as a test of the control of the men and women at the table, resolving the argument between the young woman and the colonel.
4. because she did not move
5. The woman was right. It was a woman, Mrs. Wynnes, who showed tremendous self-control.

Vocabulary

Vocabulary Building: Using Paraphrases, *page 88*

1. spirited = lively; outgrown = changed (became more mature); era = period of time
2. summons = calls; whispers = speaks very softly
3. comes to with a start = is suddenly on the alert; bait = food used to attract an animal
4. first impulse = immediate reaction (without thinking); commotion = chaos, noise; striking = attacking
5. arresting = having a quality that stops things; sobers = makes people become serious
6. forfeit = lose, give up
7. emerge = come out; make for = move towards

Vocabulary Review, *pages 88–89*

1. outgrown
2. commotion
3. emerge, bait
4. impulse

Text Analysis, *page 89*

1. The setting: a dinner party in colonial India hosted by Mr. and Mrs. Wynnes; a spacious dining room with doors leading to a veranda
2. The characters: the colonel (opinionated male chauvinist), young girl (disagrees with the colonel), the naturalist (knowledgeable, clever and controlled), Mrs. Wynnes (cool, calm, and collected)
3. The events in the **plot** are:
   - the argument between the Colonel and the young lady
   - Mrs. Wyness' awareness of the presence of the snake, leading her to have a servant place a bowl of milk on the veranda
   - the American naturalist's challenge to guests to keep still
   - successful isolation of the snake on the veranda
   - It is revealed that the snake was crawling over Mrs. Wynnes' foot.

   The **conflict** operates on two levels: 1. the discussion regarding women's behavior, and 2. the tension caused by the danger to the guests' safety. The **climax** is probably during the five minutes of silence including the emergence of the snake. The **resolution** is the safety of everyone present plus the resolution of the argument between the young woman and the Colonel when Mrs. Wynnes proves the Colonel wrong (¶10–12).

4. All the elements are necessary to make the story's point. The setting has to be in a place that has cobras at a time when men had a sense of superiority. The characters are important, but they seem to be present only to allow the plot to develop and to prove the point. Characters aren't usually well developed in such a short story. The plot is probably the most important element because it cleverly operates at two levels: the discussion and the snake crisis. All the elements are rather simply stated. Perhaps the really important thing is disproving the idea that women are less able to handle acute stress and have less self-control than men.

Unit Wrap-Up

Word Families, *pages 90–91*

1. abnormal, abnormally
2. bore
3. energetic
4. estimated
5. exhausting
6. immunization, immunize
7. relaxation, relaxing
8. relief, relieved
9. sedate
10. tranquilizer, tranquil

Polysemous Words, *pages 91–93*

1. b, a, b, c, d
2. d, a, c, b
3. a, b, a
4. b, a, c, c, b
5. b, c, a, d
6. b, a, c
7. b, c, d, a

UNIT 4 — CULTURES IN CONTACT

CHAPTER 13 — Culture

Before You Read

Previewing, *page 95*

define culture, give examples of how cultures differ

Read, *pages 95–97*

a, a, b, b, a, a, b, a, a

Comprehension Check

First Reading, *page 97*

1. Culture, as an anthropologist defines it, is the total way of life: the social legacy acquired from one's group, the part of the environment that is the creation of humans, and the "blueprint for all of life's activities." We learn our culture by being brought up in it.
2. All humans are biologically similar and go through the same physical changes from birth to death. As a result, cultures deal with the same stages of life and major events that mark them (¶9, gloss 8).

Second Reading, *page 98*

1. T (¶1)
2. F (¶2)
3. F (¶3)
4. T (¶4)
5. F (¶5)
6. T (¶6)
7. F (¶ 7, 8)
8. T (¶9)

Vocabulary

Vocabulary Building, *pages 98–99*

Part 1:

1. c
2. e
3. d
4. a
5. b

Part 2:

6. h
7. j
8. l
9. k
10. g
11. i
12. f

Using Paraphrases, *page 99*

1. selfish = caring only about yourself; undesirous of = not wanting; feminine companionship = the company of (other) women; restrict = limit; mate = sexual partner
2. orphaned = left without parents (because his parents died); infancy = when one is a young baby; reared = raised or brought up; remote = far away, not near any city
3. indignation = anger; nonrational = unreasonable; standardized unreason = regularized rule that is not logical or reasonable

84 *World of Reading 3 Teacher's Manual*

Vocabulary Review, *page 100*

1. legacy, infancy
2. standardized
3. modes, bewildered
4. restrict, abhorrent
5. undergo

Text Analysis

Text Organization:
Paragraph Purpose, *page 100*

¶1–2: define culture

¶3: states the idea that a given culture predicts a good deal of human behavior

¶4–8: provide specific examples

¶9: states that despite differences in culture, all humans are biologically similar, which limits differences among cultures

Word Order, *page 101*

2. A system of plural wives seems "instinctively" abhorrent to the American woman.
3. I met a young man in New York City some years ago who did not speak a word of English.
4. She gave no reply to queries.

CHAPTER 14
Touching

Before You Read

Previewing, *page 102*

1. in the Middle East; he is [North] American
2. differences in touching and spatial relationships

Read, *pages 103–106*

a, a, b, b, b, a, a, b, b, a, b, a, a

Comprehension Check

First Reading, *page 106*

1. The Arab host took Axtell's hand. Axtell was so surprised that he did not pull his hand away. He later learned that in Arab culture men holding hands was a sign of friendship and respect.
2. A bubble of personal space refers to the normal physical distance between people.

Second Reading, *page 106*

1. San Juan, Puerto Rico; Paris; Florida; London. Cooper's observations match Axtell's categories fairly well. However, France might look a bit more 'touch-oriented' based on Cooper's observations while Axtell placed France in the middle category. In Cooper's data, only Puerto Rico represents Latin American countries (and touching rules vary in different parts of Latin America).
2. The British press was irate that the Canadian official touched the Queen to "politely" and protectively guide her through a crowd. Although Canada is a "don't touch" country, this type of touching is not considered offensive. However, according to an unwritten British rule, no one touches the Queen or even shakes her hand unless she extends her hand first.
3. In the U.S. touching from elbow to shoulder on an airplane or in a crowded elevator is OK (¶9). In Japan, people avoid eye contact and retreat into themselves so that they are "touching without feeling" on crowded trains, in elevators, etc. (¶12).
4. Koreans avoid physical and eye contact. In a store, for example, change is not placed directly in the other person's hand; it is put on the counter. Americans find this cold and unfriendly (¶10–11).
5. A game in which a Latin moves closer to a North American or a person from Northern Europe and the American or European backs off until he or she is in a corner.
6. Even in "don't touch" countries such as the U.S., politicians "press flesh." Leo Buscaglia advocates "the joy of hugging." Cross-culturally there is accommodation to the culture, such as Japanese businessmen in the U.S. tolerating touching.
7. Liv Ullman hugged her Bangladeshi hostess. When she inquired why the woman withdrew from her hug, she learned the local rule and immediately adapted by kissing the woman's feet. They then hugged. Thus they demonstrated that we can be gracious, flexible, and willing to change.

Vocabulary

Vocabulary Building: Using Paraphrases, *page 107*

1. protests = strong complaints; row = angry argument
2. innocuous = harmless or innocent; misconstrued = misunderstood; linger = stay (for a time)
3. sexual harassment = unwanted sexual advances; accused = said to be guilty of; molestation = sexually abusing
4. unanimous = everyone agreed (100% agreement)
5. colliding = in conflict; dilemma = problem (involving making a decision)
6. ignore = not pay attention to; retreating = pulling back or into
7. steely resolve = strong determination
8. touring = traveling; famine-stricken = suffering extreme hunger; on behalf of = as a representative of
9. quintessential = a perfect example of; unhesitatingly = without stopping to think
10. parting ritual = traditional way to say good-bye

Vocabulary Review, *page 108*

1. codes
2. invade, aloof
3. collide, dilemma
4. jerk, rituals
5. reject

Text Analysis, *pages 108–109*

1. "I quickly learned that it was a world of extremes—important extremes—with some cultures seeking bodily contact and others studiously avoiding it." (¶4)
2. "Can the casual act of touching be all that important? The answer is 'yes' . . . " (¶7)
3. "Yet there are strange contradictions, especially in the United States." (¶9)
4. "Cultures are colliding every day over this dilemma of 'to touch or not to touch.'" (¶10)
5. ". . . we learn that some cultural bubbles are larger or smaller than others." (¶14)
6. "But even as these words are written, touch codes are changing all over the world." (¶15)

CHAPTER 15
Change of Heart

Before You Read

Previewing, *page 110*

1. She believed they could not get along; very negative.
2. She became friendlier with her neighbors.
3. a major change in outlook or attitude

Read, *pages 110–112*

b, a, b, a, b, a, a

Comprehension Check

First Reading, *page 112*

1. an affordable (not too expensive) neighborhood that many immigrants were moving into
2. Her attitude changed from negative to positive, triggered by the loss of her job and the ending of a relationship.
3. She had misjudged her neighbors and had neglected to see them as individuals.

Second Reading, *page 112*

1. She had prejudices and negative stereotypes and figured they could never get along. She thought that immigrants should assimilate and comply with her values. She didn't take the trouble to find out about what they were like as individuals.
2. The neighbors saw her as the unfriendly gringa who lived in the nicest house in the neighborhood.
3. She didn't like noise (rooster, loud music), advertisements in Spanish, Spanish-speaking salespeople who didn't understand her at Radio Shack, and that the supermarket didn't carry products she wanted.
4. She called the Animal Regulation Department about the rooster and the police about the loud music.
5. She learned their personal stories. For example: the woman from El Salvador who left with her two daughters when her husband was murdered; the father from Mexico who worked his way up the economic ladder—as many immigrants do. She realized they were good people who wanted the same things she did. She saw the universals that all humans have in common.

6. She finally became friendly with her neighbors, exchanging gifts at Christmas time and helping each other (such as Angel, the Guatemalan who used his jumper cables to start her car).
7. a. The problem is that she doesn't get along with her neighbors. She is the only gringa in a neighborhood of immigrants. She is biased, prejudiced, and thinks they should assimilate. Tensions, or conflict, stem from differences in values with regard to noise levels (loud music, roosters) and the fact that she reports her neighbors to the authorities.
   b. The turning point comes with the loss of her job and the end of her relationship with the man she loved (¶8).
   c. The resolution involves her learning about her neighbors, connecting with them, and becoming friends.

Vocabulary

Vocabulary Building, page 113

Part 1:

1. b	3. d	5. a
2. c	4. f	6. e

Part 2:

7. i	10. g	13. j
8. l	11. h	
9. k	12. m	

Vocabulary Review, page 114

1. prejudices, harmony
2. restore
3. grief, vulnerable
4. neglected
5. preconceived

Text Analysis, page 114

1. It's personal and inspired by something that happened to Mary Fischer, leading her to examine a social issue.
2. immigration, the assimilation of immigrants, how host country citizens treat immigrants (from the point of view of a citizen of the host country), getting along in interethnic neighborhoods
3. She concludes that host country citizens and immigrants can get along when they get to know each other.

4. She may have written this to inform the public that not everyone should have to reach their low point to learn to get along with neighbors from other countries. She is showing that people can admit errors and change. Her purpose may be to pass on the lesson she learned. She may also have been relieving her own guilt.

Chapter 16
Assembly Line

Read, pages 115–123

Part 1:

b, a, a, b, b, a, b, a, b, b, a, a, a, b, b

Part 2:

a, a

Comprehension Check, pages 123–124

Part 1:

1. to bring capitalism to rural Mexico
2. mainly by subsistence farming, supplementing his income through the sale of the baskets
3. The baskets are works of art. The designs are not painted on; they are woven into the basket. Each is a one-of-a-kind item that takes more than 20–30 hours to make (not including the time to gather the raw materials), yet people treat them as worthless. They use them to hold jewelry, flowers, and little dolls (¶7). They apparently don't appreciate the Indian's talent.
4. Townspeople were nasty and rude to the Indian. They treated him like a beggar and insulted him (¶15). They bargained to get the lowest price and even then tried to cheat him by saying they didn't have change. Clearly, they looked down on Indians who were at the bottom of the socio-economic ladder.
5. as a potential source of profit
6. Mr. Winthrop
7. Mr. Winthrop assumes that the larger the quantity someone buys, the lower the price, which underlies the concept of mass production.
8. Mr. Winthrop and Mr. Kemple each try to get the best deal possible for themselves. They pretend to have little interest and don't show enthusiasm. Kemple delays making a decision and makes demands on

Mr. Winthrop (variety and exclusivity). Winthrop acts like there is competition and the deal will go to the highest bidder.

Part 2:

9. Mr. Winthrop proposes that the Indian make 10,000 baskets. As the intermediary, Winthrop will make a lot more money than the Indian.
10. The Indian remains calm, as usual, saying he can make as many baskets as Winthrop wants, but there is no way he can make 10,000 baskets in a limited time; he is not an assembly line for mass production, something that Mr. Winthrop does not understand. Consequently, they cannot reach an agreement.
11. On the economic level, Winthrop cannot understand how the price goes up as the quantity goes up (contradictory to mass production). On the artistic level, he cannot appreciate that the Indian's soul is woven into each basket and that the Indian will not compromise his way of making them.
12. The Indian does not understand mass production. Artistry and mass production are incompatible. Nevertheless, Mr. Winthrop is demanding mass production as on an assembly line.

Vocabulary

Vocabulary Building, *pages 124–125*

Part 1:
1. d   3. b   5. c
2. f   4. a   6. e

Part 2:
7. k   9. g   11. h
8. l   10. i   12. j

Synonyms, *pages 125–126*

1. a, b   5. b, c   9. a, c
2. b, c   6. a, c   10. b, c
3. a, c   7. a, c
4. a, c   8. a, b

Vocabulary Review, *page 126*

1. peasant, accomplished
2. exquisite, peddles
3. bargain, nasty
4. mission, assorted
5. despair
6. sake, grasp

Text Analysis, *page 127*

AREAS OF DIFFERENCE	MR. WINTHROP	INDIAN
a. occupation	business man	peasant/subsistence farmer, artist/basketmaker
b. personality	pushy, rude, self-centered	quiet, calm, humble, honest, intelligent
c. communication style	hard-driving, pushy, not particularly polite (curses)	very polite and respectful, calm
d. aim in life	to get rich	to get by as a farmer and to make baskets as a form of artistic expression
Possible additions		
values, view of art	materialistic, totally misses the point of art for art's sake	values art rather than money, weaves his soul into it
world view	urban, industrialized, thinks he understands rural Mexico within 3 weeks	little knowledge of the outside world
education	probably college-educated	probably little or no formal education

1. Winthrop represents the urban, unthinking capitalistic world while the Indian represents the rural peasant and artist.
2. Traven comes across as anti-American (perhaps the reason he lived in Mexico) and anti-capitalist (perhaps the reason his work was neglected in the U.S.). He admires the Indian and recognizes how badly treated he is by Mexican townspeople and by Winthrop, who wants to take advantage of him. Thus, Traven is sympathetic toward the Indian and critical of Winthrop, whose character is almost a caricature or satire of the culturally insensitive, greedy American businessman.

Unit Wrap-Up

Word Families, *pages 128–129*

1. assimilate, assimilation
2. assortment
3. bewildered, bewildering
4. collided, collision
5. comply
6. confrontational, confrontation
7. harmoniously
8. hesitate
9. indignant
10. invasion

Collocations, *pages 129–130*

1. thinking/thought/expression/behavior/transportation
2. transportation
3. chance/possibility
4. village/region/area
5. peace/order/democracy/civil rights
6. devastation/confusion/despair/misery
7. confusion/darkness
8. rose/came/were brought
9. on, below/beneath

UNIT 5 ETHICS

CHAPTER 17
Treasures from Troy

Before You Read

Previewing, *page 132*

1. Pierce defines ethics as rules for distinguishing between right and wrong.
2. This reading will illustrate the third definition: "a method, procedure, or perspective for deciding how to act."

Read, *pages 133–135*

b, b, a, a, a, b, a, b, b

Comprehension Check

First Reading, *page 135*

1. The issue is whether or not to accept the exam stolen from the professor's computer.
2. The main question is, "What will happen to me?"
3. "How would I feel if I were in the place of others (affected by my action)?"
4. "How will I look if this action is made public?"

Second Reading, *page 136*

1. T (¶6), row 1, column 1 of the chart
2. T (¶7), row 2, column 1 of the chart
3. T (¶8), row 3, column 1 of the chart
4. F row 1, column 2 of the chart
5. T row 2, column 2 of the chart
6. F row 3, column 2 of the chart

Vocabulary

Vocabulary Building, *page 136*

1. e
2. d
3. i
4. h
5. a
6. j
7. g
8. b
9. c
10. f

Student Book Answer Key 89

Multiword Expressions, *page 137*

1. found out
2. hack into
3. shed (some) light on
4. get caught
5. get away with
6. bring (these) out into the open
7. traded places
8. cut a deal
9. cover all the (ethics) bases
10. figured out

Vocabulary Review, *pages 137–138*

1. alternatives
2. hack into
3. reflect on, get away with, expelled
4. trade places
5. horrified
6. implicate
7. controversial

Text Analysis, *page 138*

1. a. ¶1: a definition of ethics
   b. ¶3: a scenario for analysis
   c. "defining ethics," "airtight definition"
   d. "Doing ethics is unavoidable. So let's begin with an example."
2. It connects back to ¶3. The words that make the connection are "in situations like this."
3. ¶5 points forward and names the three ethics tests, leading into the descriptions of the tests in ¶6–8.

CHAPTER 18
Why You Shouldn't Do It

Before You Read

Previewing, *page 139*

1. copying and distributing copyrighted music illegally
2. to discourage stealing and to protect the rights of songwriters, artists, and record companies by presenting the issue from the point of view of the music industry

Read, *pages 140–142*

b, a, b, a

Comprehension Check

First Reading, *page 142*

2. Stealing music hurts and shows disloyalty to songwriters and performers.
3. It hurts the careers of new music groups and individual artists.
4. It affects other related jobs down to employees in record stores.

Second Reading, *page 142*

1. to promote science and useful arts (¶4, quote from Constitution)
2. Recording artists are rich (¶5). It's a victimless crime (¶9).
3. When people take a product without paying for it, they are saying they do not value it. The creators are taking a risk and adding value; they must be compensated for this.
4. for publicity, but they risk it being copied illegally and losing their investment
5. Producing an album can cost the recording company more than a million dollars, and only 1 in 10 is profitable (¶10).
6. The livelihood of everyone in the industry is in danger. The artists whose music you are copying will have less chance of success.

Vocabulary

Vocabulary Building: Synonyms, *page 143*

1. a, c
2. b, c
3. a, b
4. a, c
5. b, c
6. a, c
7. b, c
8. a, c
9. a, b
10. b, c
11. a, b
12. a, b
13. a, c
14. a, c

Multiword Expressions, *page 144*

2. do the best job possible, do something perfectly
3. making a living, staying out of debt (not drowning in debt)
4. beginning, new and likely to be successful and popular
5. a crime that doesn't hurt anyone
6. is stopped, is cut short, comes to an end
7. makes money
8. getting fans, becoming known
9. provide or invest the money

Vocabulary Review, *page 145*

1. distribution
2. granted
3. burn, copyright
4. betray, threaten (Although the first blank could be filled with "threaten" it is needed for the 2nd blank.)
5. up-and-coming

Text Analysis

Supporting General Statements, *page 145*

1. ¶8: The author compares reproducing and distributing copyrighted material without permission to robbing your neighbor, which you wouldn't do, not only because of criminal penalties, but because most people consider stealing wrong.
2. ¶2, 13: It harms musicians, stores, and all aspects of the business.
3. ¶5–7: Taking something and saying it should be free is like saying it has no value. It is disloyal to the artists who work hard to produce something when we aren't willing to pay for it.
4. ¶9–10: The company can't promote the careers of new artists if they don't make money from recordings. The companies need the income to promote the artists' careers.
5. ¶13: The author points out the consequences for all people in any aspect of the music industry.

Author's Purpose, *page 146*

c. to persuade

CHAPTER 19
A Plea for the Chimps

Before You Read

Previewing, *page 147*

1. Chimps and humans are similar genetically, in physiology, biochemistry, in their immune system, and in their behavior, psychology, and emotions.
2. Goodall requests that we consider the ethical question raised in ¶2 and that we speak for the chimps as they cannot speak for themselves (¶46).

Read, *pages 148–154*

Part 1:

b, a, b, a, b, a, b, b, a, b

Part 2:

a, a, a, b, a, b, a, a, b, b, b, a, a

Comprehension Check, *page 154*

Part 1:

1. because they are so similar to humans (¶1)
2. She actually poses two questions but focuses on the second one.
   First, are we justified in using an animal so close to us—an animal, moreover, that is highly endangered in its African forest home—as a human substitute in medical experimentation? (¶2) Second, how are we treating the chimpanzees that are actually being used? (¶7) This is the only question we can do something about now without facing the ethical issue raised by her first question.
3. ¶8–14 describe horrible conditions, including the following facts: the chimps are housed alone in cages that are too small and allow for none of their normal activity and movement; the chimps can't even lie down. There is nothing comfortable. There is nothing for them to do (¶25–26).
4. Chimps in their natural habitat are sociable, active, and playful (¶16–21). They enjoy comfort, are very intelligent, empathize with other chimps and do things for other chimps. They show human-like emotions like happiness, fear, anger, and even have a sense of humor.

Part 2:

5. They are isolated in small spaces with no stimulation or comfort, a dramatic contrast with their lifestyle in the forest.
6. If veterinarians fight for more humane conditions, they may be excluded from the labs (¶30).
7. Some of them do quit because they cannot tolerate the conditions, but others are desensitized and become callous (¶29).
8. Some scientists believe these conditions are necessary for the treatment to be carried out. They also claim that with more space the chimps might hurt themselves. Objects in the cages such as toys or bedding make the cages harder to clean, and the chimps might get parasites or diseases. Isolation is necessary to avoid cross infection (¶31–34).

9. Goodall suggests that scientists may be wrong because depressed, isolated chimps are more likely to get sick. Also, if treated better, they will be more cooperative (¶37, 41).
10. Goodall suggests increasing the number of trained caretakers who spend time with the chimps and are present when chimps are receiving treatment; with this change, the chimps would suffer less stress. They could also have an animal from a compatible species as a companion. As for cage size, she suggests following the laws already in place in Switzerland. In addition to space, chimps need climbing apparatus and other stimulating objects so they have some control over their environment (¶36–42).
11. CHIMP Act (2000) calls for refuge camps for retired laboratory chimps instead of killing them after experiments are finished. Because some research can be done with human cells instead of live animals, the number of projects involving primates has been cut in half. However, in 2005 there were still about 1,300 chimps in research labs.

Vocabulary

Vocabulary Building, pages 155–156

Part 1:

1. d	5. g	9. f
2. c	6. a	10. i
3. b	7. h	
4. j	8. e	

Part 2:

11. p	14. m	17. k
12. n	15. l	18. o
13. q	16. r	

Vocabulary Review, pages 156–157

1. bleak (could also be "miserable," but "miserable" is needed for question 8)
2. confined, despair
3. bonds
4. alleviating
5. compassionate
6. isolation
7. stimulating
8. miserable

Text Analysis, page 157

Introduction (¶1–7)

a. the use and treatment of chimps in labs for medical research
b. 1. Are we justified in using chimps in medical experiments knowing what we do about chimps? 2. How are we treating the chimpanzees that are actually being used (while we are waiting for alternatives)?
c. She gets readers interested by showing how similar chimps are to humans.

Body (¶8–43)

¶8–14: describes Goodall's visit to the NIH lab

¶15: transitions from description of dismal conditions in NIH lab to a description of the nature of the chimpanzees in their natural habitat

¶16–23: describes the true nature of chimps, their natural characteristics

¶24–26: describes how the conditions in most labs contradict the true nature of chimps

¶27: transitions from lab conditions to discussion of the views of humans who work there

¶28–34: discusses how the humans (caretakers, veterinarians, scientists) who work in these labs view the situation

¶35–43: makes suggestions for improving conditions

Conclusion (¶44–46)

¶44–45: points out hopeful signs

¶46: discusses Goodall's personal connection to chimps and the reason she makes this plea

CHAPTER 20
The Wallet

Read, pages 159–160

b, b, a, b, a

Comprehension Check, pages 160–161

1. Elaine is a tollbooth worker.
2. Troy is Elaine's co-worker.
3. Troy works the shift before Elaine's night shift.
4. Elaine doesn't particularly appreciate Troy, especially when he leaves things for her to clean up and harasses her.
5. Elaine finds the job boring and tries to find ways to entertain herself.

6. *Answers will vary.* This looks like a case of domestic abuse. The woman must be leaving her husband/partner and taking her two children with her. She might not have any money of her own, or she might have left home in a hurry and forgotten to take money.
7. Elaine saw movement in the backseat of the car and quickly noticed that the children's eyes were wide open and frightened-looking.
8. She gives her the money in Troy's wallet, which he left in her tollbooth (presumably so he would have an excuse to come back and talk to or flirt with Elaine).

Vocabulary

Vocabulary Building: Using Paraphrases, *page 161*

1. deliberately = on purpose; retrieved = got back
2. awkward small talk = uncomfortable conversation about unimportant things; cramped = small, crowded
3. stool = high seat; shift = 8 hours of work; lingering = continuing
4. lecherous type = guy who only thought about women as sex objects
5. screeched = made a high, loud, unpleasant sound; roared = made a deep, very loud sound; pocked with rust = covered with reddish spots where paint was gone
6. bleary = tired, unclear, teary; splotched = covered with marks
7. gash = ugly cut; swollen up = gotten puffy
8. stare = unchanging look on her face; bitter and bold = angry and confident

Vocabulary Review, *page 162*

The averbs may appear to be interchangeable, but answers should follow the facts of the story.

1. shift
2. annoying, maid
3. deliberately
4. screeched
5. gripping
6. swollen
7. held up, surreptitiously

Text Analysis, *page 163*

NAME	PHYSICAL DESCRIPTION	PERSONALITY
Troy		manipulative and lecherous, left unfinished drinks as though Elaine were his servant, left his wallet as an excuse to come back
Elaine		someone who takes control and tries to make the most of a situation, knows what she likes and doesn't like, tries to make the boring night shift more interesting by counting cars, sees drivers who don't pull up close enough as an excuse to stretch; she puts Troy's leftover drink in the wastebasket upright so it won't spill and lines up coins in neat rows; these are details which show she's tidy
Woman in the car	stringy hair, gash under one eye, swollen black eye, splotches on her face, scar on her nose, blood in the corner of her mouth; these details allow readers to infer the woman's situation; knowing the situation is important in evaluating Elaine's decision to give her Troy's money	

Unit Wrap-Up

Word Families, *pages 164–165*

1. appreciation
2. compassionately
3. controversy, controversial
4. deceptive, deceive
5. deliberate (*adj.*), deliberate (*v.*)
6. infectious
7. isolated (*v.*)
8. rationalize
9. scandalous
10. threaten, threateningly

Collocations, *pages 165–166*

1. pain/suffering/stress/tension
2. noise/sound/background music
3. a wheelchair/the house/bed/a hospital
4. waving/shouting/calling
5. weather
6. politics/the game
7. issues/points/ethical questions/doubts
8. conversation/discussion
9. discussion/participation/interest

UNIT 6 — THE ENVIRONMENT

CHAPTER 21
Humans and Sustainability: An Overview

Before You Read

Previewing, *page 168*

1. Part 1: Figure 1—exponential population growth; Figure 2—what nature gives us; Figure 3—the ecological footprint showing that we are living unsustainably
   Part 2: Figure 4—how we should use what we get from nature
2. environment, environmental science, sustainability or durability, natural capital, solar capital, environmentally sustainable society, environmental worldview, environmental ethics, planetary management worldview, stewardship worldview, environmental wisdom worldview; The terms are set in boldface green in the text.
3. a, b, c, e

Read, *pages 169–174*

Part 1:

b, a, a, a, b, a, b, a, b, a

Part 2:

b, a, b, b, a, b, b, a

Comprehension Check

First Reading, *pages 174–175*

Part 1:

A. 1. the sum total of all living and non-living things that affect any living organism
   2. affects the environment
   3. interdisciplinary, natural, social
   4. a

B. 2, 4, 5, 6, 8

Part 2:

1. Both, depending on one's point of view or outlook.
2. planetary management worldview, stewardship worldview, environmental wisdom worldview
3. 50–100 years at most

Second Reading, *pages 175–176*

Part 1:

1. T (¶4), figure 2
2. T (¶5)
3. F (¶6)
4. F (¶7)
5. T (¶9)
6. F (subhead), (¶11–14)
7. T (¶14; more evidence in Part 2, ¶16)

94 *World of Reading 3 Teacher's Manual*

Part 2:
1. F (¶15–16)
2. T (¶18)
3. F (¶19)
4. T (¶21)
5. T (¶22)
6. T (¶23)
7. F (¶26, 27)

Vocabulary

Vocabulary Building, pages 176–177

Part 1:
1. f
2. d
3. e
4. b
5. g
6. a
7. c

Part 2:
8. m
9. l
10. k
11. h
12. i
13. j

Word Analysis, pages 177–178

1. a. affect (each other); verb that has to do with action or behavior between two things (humans and the earth, in this case)
   b. involving two or more different areas of study
   c. between or among different religions
2. a. secondary (below the primary) themes or topics
   b. below water (ships that go under water)
3. a. treating everyone equally
   b. consider that one thing is the same as (equal to) something else
   c. the same distance from two (or more) places
4. a. final (in the end)
   b. final comment or threat (last or final chance)
5. a. broke, with no money (bank is broken)
   b. breaking the continuity of something
   c. break into a conversation or activity, stop it from continuing
6. a. new ideas, methods, inventions
   b. a person who is new at something
   c. new, different, unusual (idea)

Vocabulary Review, pages 178–179

Part 1:
1. replenish, rate, squander
2. compromises
3. banning
4. indefinitely

Part 2:
1. ingenuity, innovations
2. unsustainably, depleting
3. preserve, stabilize
4. wisdom
5. witness

Text Analysis, page 180

1. natural capital
2. living sustainably
3. living unsustainably
4. spending your capital, not just the interest or income it earns, and eventually going bankrupt

CHAPTER 22
Islands of Green

Before You Read

Previewing, page 181

1. environmentally friendly
2. cities
3. examples of cities that are going green

Read, pages 181–183

b, a, b, a, b, b, a, a

Comprehension Check

First Reading, page 183

1. Portland has reduced carbon dioxide emissions. It has turned out to be good for the economy, contrary to the prediction that it wouldn't be.
2. L.A. was losing rainfall to runoff because the city is covered with concrete. The solution was to install drains leading to gravel pits to capture and treat water.
3. production of local food and farmers' markets
4. reducing cars in the city through public transportation (buses)

5. a rainforest preserved as a national park; it will become part of a wildlife corridor system to restore biodiversity outside the city
6. reducing cars in the city
7. green housing
8. housing; apartment buildings with farms on the rooftops

Second Reading, *page 184*

2. R They went against the prevailing view.
3. R If they did not get rain, there would be no runoff to lose.
4. U L.A. "epitomizes car-dependent sprawl."
5. U There are farms in the area.
6. R They approved a referendum in 2000 declaring an annual car-free day, indicating they support public transportation and car-free days.
7. R 47% of trips are by bike; 26% are on foot (walking).
8. R The examples in Peabody, England and Johannesburg, South Africa, demonstrate that green housing can reduce the ecological footprint.
9. U There is no mention of the size of cities in China.

Vocabulary

Vocabulary Building, *page 185*

Part 1:

1. e 3. f 5. a
2. d 4. b 6. c

Part 2:

7. i 9. k 11. g
8. l 10. h 12. j

Multiword Expressions, *pages 185–186*

1. (seven years) to spare
2. around the globe
3. makes sense
4. dying of thirst
5. put . . . to shame
6. runner-up
7. pedestrian zones
8. rush hour
9. leads the way
10. fair share
11. a slew of
12. from scratch

Vocabulary Review, *pages 186–187*

1. scattered
2. pedestrian zones, amenities
3. carbon emissions, wreck
4. capture
5. infrastructure
6. fair share
7. makes sense

Text Analysis, *page 187*

1. It is a list and has no conclusion.
2. The body is an expanded list. The sections are headed by the names of a city followed by a paragraph about each.
3. The author wants to give us examples of ways cities are going green. We have a list of cities with a paragraph explaining what they have done or are doing.
4. The first two sentences of ¶1 express the main idea that we have pieces of what a green city would be. (We can infer that what is really needed is cities that have all of these features together.)

CHAPTER 23

Part 1: Think You Can Be a Meat-Eating Environmentalist? Think Again!
Part 2: It's a Plastic World

Before You Read

Previewing, *page 188*

1. Both present a problem and solutions; both have lists.
2. *Answers will vary.*

Read, *pages 188–191*

Part 1:

a, b, b

Part 2:

a, a, b, a

Comprehension Check

First Reading, *pages 191–192*

Part 1:

1. T (¶1, 5)	4. T (¶3)	7. F (¶7)
2. T (¶2)	5. T (¶4)	8. F (¶8)
3. F (¶2)	6. F (¶6)	

Part 2:

1. F (¶4), 1st bullet
2. T (¶2, 4), 2nd bullet
3. T (¶4), 3rd bullet, box at end
4. F (¶4), 4th bullet
5. T (¶3, 5, 7), step 2
6. T (¶7), step 4
7. T (¶7), step 5

Second Reading, *pages 192–193*

Part 1:

1. R McCartney's quote endorsing vegetarianism
2. R It overuses resources such as land, water, and energy without replenishing them.
3. U Water pollution of rivers and lakes spread to other areas (¶2). ¶6 refers to uncontained pollution of the oceans.
4. R Growing grain for livestock uses more land, water, and energy than growing food for a vegetarian diet (¶3–5).
5. U Fish farms pollute and fishing practices kill a lot of bycatch (¶8). It is doubtful that the author would recommend fish (even if it's healthy) because of other damage the fish industry causes.
6. U There is no mention of hunting these species, but it is mentioned that they are bycatch (¶6).
7. R There is no mention of transportation, but it can be inferred to be part of the energy used by the meat industry (¶5).
8. R We can infer that if these types of food are available, there is a market for them (¶8).

Part 2:

1. U (¶4), 2nd bullet
2. U (subhead), (¶6), 1st bullet; Bottled water comes in plastic bottles, so it's unreasonable that anti-plastic authors would recommend it.
3. R (¶6), first bullet, (¶7), Step 2, 5
4. U (¶7), Step 3
5. R (¶7), Step 5
6. R (¶7), Step 4

Vocabulary

Vocabulary Building, *pages 193–194*

Part 1:

1. g	4. b	7. c
2. d	5. h	8. e
3. f	6. a	

Part 2:

1. i	5. c	9. d
2. g	6. h	10. a
3. e	7. b	
4. j	8. f	

Vocabulary Review, *pages 194–195*

Part 1:

1. livestock
2. emissions
3. marine
4. horrible
5. counter, scale

Part 2:

1. drawbacks
2. disposable
3. durability
4. concept, winds up
5. cut down on
6. overnight

Text Analysis, *page 195*

1. Part 1 has boldface titles indicating the topic of the following paragraph. The list in Part 1 includes shocking facts. Part 2 has several types of lists: bulleted lists in ¶4, 6 and a list of steps in ¶7. The first bulleted list provides facts that are not commonly known. The second bulleted list and the list of steps indicate things people can do.
2. Lists make it easy to see what is included and are easy to read.
3. *Answers will vary.*
4. *Answers will vary.* Part 1 makes the topics very clear while Part 2, which is longer, has a more complex format.

Student Book Answer Key **97**

CHAPTER 24
Prayer for the Great Family

Comprehension Check

First Reading, *page 197*

1. earth/soil, plants, air, wild beings/animals, water (including clouds, leading to rain, and glaciers), sun, sky
2. "The Great Family" refers to all of nature/natural capital. Snyder certainly seems to hold the environmental wisdom worldview that we are merely a part of and dependent upon nature, just like any other species.

Second Reading, *page 197*

Possible answers might include the following:

1. The poet describes each aspect of nature listed in First Reading, question 1. The images are predominantly visual (plants are "sun-facing light-changing leaf"; "their dance is in the flowing spiral grain"; the Sun's light is "blinding pulsing light through trunks of trees, through mists . . ."). There are also occasional suggestions of smell (the soil smells "sweet"), sound ("breath of our song" "clear spirit breathes"), and touch.
2. The aspects of the environment dealt with in each stanza cover natural capital as defined in chapter 21: air, water, soil/land, life (plants and animals), sun, and wind.
3. Humans should be grateful for nature's services and the things Mother Earth has given us.
4. The Great Sky refers to the whole universe (possibly God). Snyder comments that we are part of it; many people believe that God is within us ("yet is within us"). He renames the Great Sky "Grandfather Space" and he says the "Mind" (the minds of humans) is Grandfather Space's wife, implying a close connection between humans and the universe.

Unit Wrap-Up

Word Families, *pages 198–199*

1. compensation
2. disposable
3. diversity
4. durable
5. grateful
6. miracle
7. pollution, unpolluted
8. sustain
9. wise

Polysemous Words, *pages 199–200*

1. d, a, b, e, c
2. b, a
3. b, b, a, c
4. d, a, c, b, a
5. g, e, c, a, b, f, d
6. b, a

Unit Tests

Test Rationale

Although tests are required as a means of evaluation by educational institutions, their primary purpose should be to solidify learning. Since language learning is a long-term endeavor, tests should be viewed as another opportunity for students to improve reading ability and knowledge of vocabulary.

The tests in this series, therefore, have two goals. First, they provide feedback to both students and teachers on how well students have understood and begun to learn the material of a unit. Second, they give students an opportunity to apply their developing reading abilities to new material.

A corollary of this testing philosophy is that only teachers who are in regular contact with the developing skills of their students are capable of judging the fairness of any test. Thus, teachers should alter tests as they see fit for their particular students or teaching situations.

Test Format

PART 1: REVIEWING (Unit Content)

Paragraph Completion

These exercises, which are similar to the Vocabulary Review in each unit, check students' knowledge of vocabulary items that are central to the content of the unit. Completing cloze exercises correctly depends on knowing both the meaning of the vocabulary items and how they express the central ideas of the readings.

Word Families

These exercises are similar to the word family exercises in the Unit Wrap-Up. They require students to select the correct grammatical form of a word for a new context. They call attention to the suffixes that are commonly associated with the categories of nouns, verbs, adjectives and adverbs, and contribute to developing accuracy in both speaking and writing.

Matching

The matching sections emphasize that knowing a word is more than knowing its meanings; it is also a matter of knowing how native speakers combine words to form multiword expressions and common combinations of words, i.e. collocations.

Writing

These questions check students' developing abilities to learn from what they read, an important academic skill. They also help students develop as writers and test takers by offering regular opportunities to write short answers to questions about the readings they have done. Students should gradually get better at writing clear, focused answers. Teachers should decide whether they want to evaluate only the content of answers or both the content and grammatical accuracy of the writing.

There are several ways to prepare students to do well on this section. In the beginning, the questions may be given to students ahead of time to discuss in small groups. Teachers can also add a couple of other questions so that students don't know the exact choice they will have on the test. Over a period of time, advance knowledge of the questions could be eliminated so students experience the reality of test taking as it is in many college courses.

Part 2: EXPLORING (New Reading)

The goal of *World of Reading* is to enable students to read authentic texts written for native English speakers. Therefore, new readings similar in level to those in the Student Book are part of each test, giving students an opportunity to read additional authentic material, not with the idea of preparing it for class, but with the idea of obtaining as much information from it as possible.

Vocabulary

Although the vocabulary items all look alike, there are two kinds of items: 1. those where the meaning of the word is inferable from context (similar to the marginal multiple choice items in the *Student Book*) and 2. those where there really isn't enough context. In the latter case, items are designed to encourage students to check that a meaning makes sense. To accomplish this, there are two obviously incorrect distracters; if students are paying attention, this provides the meaning of the target word or expression, as only one choice makes sense. This is preferable to giving students the definitions as glosses because it encourages intelligent thinking and closer attention to the text. A few items, however, are glossed.

Comprehension

Finally, students demonstrate how much of the new selection they are able to understand. In most cases, this is done through true/false items. When you go over the test with students, encourage them to identify the evidence that helped them answer each question. Be sure they understand why the false statements are false.

In the case of some readings, the content does not lend itself to ten good true/false items, so students answer *Wh*-questions to demonstrate their understanding.

Name: _____   Date: _____

UNIT 1 FRIENDSHIP

PART ONE
REVIEWING

1.1 Paragraph Completion (10 points)

Complete the paragraph with items from the list. Use each item only once.

| critical | exposure | intensity | keeping up with | peers |
| enrich | furthermore | intersect | ongoing | promotes |

Friends are important; they (1) _____ our lives from childhood through old age. We make friends with people whose lives (2) _____ with ours: children make friends with their (3) _____ in school; college students become friends with roommates and classmates, proving that proximity and (4) _____ are important factors in forming friendships. Nowadays people also make friends online though it's harder to figure out what (5) _____ friendships between people who don't meet face-to-face. Even if you don't like the idea of cyber-friends, many people find computers convenient for (6) _____ the real-world friends they already have. (7) _____, it is reassuring that with computers people can maintain (8) _____ relationships with lifelong friends even after they no longer live close to one another. Friendships vary in (9) _____ and serve different purposes, but having a couple of good friends is (10) _____ to our well-being.

1.2 Word Families (5 points)

Choose the correct form of the word to complete each sentence.

1. It's not always easy to _____ to a friend.
   a. apologetic   b. apologize   c. apology

2. It's wise to be _____ when you meet someone online.
   a. cautiously   b. cautious   c. caution

3. What you find out about a person in real life might _____ the information they give you on the Internet.
   a. contradict   b. contradictory   c. contradiction

4. Call for information about our online dating service; there's no _____ to sign up.
   a. obligatory   b. obligation   c. obligate

5. Modern medicine tries to use less _____ methods before doing major surgery.
   a. intrusion   b. intrude   c. intrusive

102   World of Reading 3 Teacher's Manual

© 2009 by Pearson Education, Inc. Duplication for classroom use is permitted.

1.3 Matching (6 points)

Match the beginning of the sentence on the left with the correct ending on the right. Use each choice only once. You will not use all of the endings.

_____ 1. Patricia would like to back out
_____ 2. Do you mean she wants to break up
_____ 3. He's so dependent on her. Will he get
_____ 4. He'll probably just hang
_____ 5. I think it will take a good deal
_____ 6. Too bad. They both have such great senses

a. of time for him to get over the breakup.
b. the way home.
c. of humor.
d. of her relationship with Paul.
e. along all right without her?
f. out more with his buddies.
g. with him?

1.4 Writing (9 points)

Answer *three* of the questions. Write two to three complete sentences for each answer, using information from the readings in the unit.

1. Discuss two categories of friends described by Judith Viorst. What purpose does the friendship serve for the two people involved? Be sure to give specific examples.
2. Do you prefer to use the computer to make friends or to enhance friendships you already have? Explain your preference in detail.
3. Proximity, exposure, similarity and physical attractiveness have been shown to be important factors in bringing people together to form friendships. In your opinion, how has technology affected at least two of these factors?
4. Why was making friends in school particularly important for Jim Davy?

PART TWO

EXPLORING

2.1 Reading

Read the text.

Friends As Healers

Old friends are good for you, physically, mentally, and emotionally.

1   The hunger for friendship begins in childhood and stays with us throughout our lives. Close friends are particularly important because they know our assets and our flaws and think we're just great anyway. Often these friendships are highly dynamic, moving through the years from tranquility to occasional discord, from intense support to lesser involvement, and back again.

2   "People who maintain a safety net of friends can protect themselves against the losses that come with age," says gerontologist[1] Rosemary Blieszner of Virginia Polytechnic Institute and State University. "The qualities that people mention in studies—confiding problems and needs, building trust, addressing problems that come up—are foundations for friendships that contribute to physical and mental health."

3   Confiding in someone may offer big payoffs in terms of health, experts say. A Stanford University School of Medicine study, published in 1989, compared two groups of women

---
[1]**gerontologist** a doctor specializing in old age

with metastatic breast cancer: those who attended regular support meetings, and those who toughed it out on their own. The pain levels among those who attended meetings were significantly lower than their counterparts. The meetings also helped alleviate stress and depression. The best news? Survival rates for the supported women were nearly twice as high.

4 "The willingness to disclose our deepest feelings to another person has an effect on the central nervous system that affects the cardiovascular[2] and immune systems,"[3] says Blair Justice, associate dean of academic affairs and professor of psychology at the University of Texas—Houston School of Public Health.

5 When we don't confide our problems, Justice says, the body and brain work overtime to suppress[4] emotions. Disclosing our feelings is an act of release, which reduces stress hormones that dampen, or reduce, immune response and hike, that is increase, blood pressure. "It's very stressful on the body to constantly repress feelings," says Justice.

6 How many friends do you need before your health improves? "Much benefit can be had from a warm, close relationship with just one other person," Justice says. "Quality is more important than quantity."

7 And the quality is often highest when it comes from a woman, Blieszner says. "Both men and women feel closer to females who give support. Women are more relational and listen to problems and give feedback. They have deeper relationships. Some use the expression, 'Men have side-by-side friendships; women have face-to-face friendships.' Men's friendships are activity-based; women want to talk about things. That's true across all ages."

8 In fact, husbands rely almost exclusively on their spouses to fulfill intimacy needs. Wives do not. In surveys, men routinely list their spouses as being their best friends.

9 While men may feel their greatest support from women friends, cross-gender friendships prove to be the hardest to maintain. "Opposite-gender friends can promote jealousy between close partners," says Robert Milardo, professor of family relationships at the University of Maine.

10 After three decades of research, the evidence is clear: Good friends are critically important to successful aging. Friends can be "more important to the psychological well-being of older adults than even family members are," according to Blieszner's research. She notes that older adults can more easily receive moral support from people their own age. Although family relationships are meaningful and family members provide important support such as health care, relationships that are built from scratch, rather than ascribed,[5] retain more importance in terms of mental and emotional health.

11 "With families, old power relationships are still there, and old baggage," says Blieszner. "But friends are age peers. They're chosen relationships." And what could be more valuable than a handpicked support network of friends to enrich your life? "The bottom line is: Friends are essential to everyone's life," Blieszner says. "Everyone needs friends."

---

[2]**cardiovascular** related to the heart and circulatory system

[3]**immune system** the system by which the body protects itself against disease

[4]**suppress** both *suppress* and *repress* in (¶5) mean hold back, not show or express

[5]**built from scratch, rather than ascribed** chosen and developed from the beginning; not due to family relationship

2.2 Vocabulary *(10 points)*

Find the underlined word or expression in the indicated paragraph. Choose the meaning that makes sense in the context.

1. our assets and our flaws (¶1) means
   a. our friends and our enemies
   b. our good points and our bad points
   c. what we have and what we owe

2. payoffs (¶3) means
   a. benefits   b. loans   c. money

3. toughed it out on their own (¶3) means
   a. did not participate in a support group
   b. liked support groups   c. were very strict

4. alleviate (¶3) means
   a. cause   b. complicate   c. reduce

5. disclose (¶4) means
   a. lie about   b. remove   c. share

6. feedback (¶7) means
   a. advice   b. favors   c. food

7. fulfill (¶8) means
   a. create   b. destroy   c. satisfy

8. jealousy (¶9) means
   a. love and affection between a man and a woman
   b. distrust and anger when another person comes between you and your partner
   c. problems related to money

9. (old) baggage (¶11) means
   a. emotional problems from the past
   b. too much weight
   c. old suitcases

10. handpicked (¶11) means
    a. small   b. made by hand   c. carefully chosen

2.3 Comprehension *(10 points)*

Mark the statements *T* (true) or *F* (false).

1. **T F** This article states that friendships are more important when we are young than when we are older.
2. **T F** Close friendships can change quite a bit over time.
3. **T F** When we share feelings and problems with a friend, we increase the effectiveness of the immune system and reduce stress.
4. **T F** Women with breast cancer who attended a support group had less stress, but the course of their disease was no different from women who did not participate in a support group.
5. **T F** The more friends you have, the bigger the health benefit.

6. **T F** Men are more likely to be special-interest friends who do things together than close friends who talk a lot about personal matters.
7. **T F** According to this article, both women and men are better able to talk about problems with women than with men.
8. **T F** According to surveys, both men and women list their spouses as their best friends.
9. **T F** According to this article, it is fairly easy for both men and women to maintain friendships with people of the opposite sex.
10. **T F** The author of this article is in agreement with Judith Viorst, who said that friends can be more important than family.

Name: _____ Date: _____

UNIT 2: PARENTS AND CHILDREN

PART ONE
REVIEWING

1.1 Paragraph Completion (10 points)

Complete the paragraphs with items from the list. Use each item only once.

| accomplish | hectic | potential | puzzled | urge |
| convince | nurture | pursue | thrive | wonder |

All children need parents or caregivers who (1) _____ them, inspire them to have confidence in themselves, and help them reach their (2) _____—as Mrs. Michelotti did. Children need people who show them that if they work hard, they can (3) _____ important things in life.

But raising children isn't easy. Daily life can be (4) _____, and there will be times when parents and children don't understand each other and (5) _____ if they will ever be able to communicate well.

Ironically, many North American parents (6) _____ children to become independent, yet they may be (7) _____ when their children leave home to (8) _____ their own plans. It was hard for a North American woman to (9) _____ José that this is why Freddy and Henry left California. Despite disagreements and misunderstandings, most parents around the world want their children to (10) _____ and live happy lives.

1.2 Word Families (5 points)

Choose the correct form of the word to complete each sentence.

1. I'm eighteen, and it _____ me when my parents treat me like a little child.
   a. furious   b. furiously   c. infuriates

2. It's hard to explain the _____ I feel when my parents won't listen to my point of view.
   a. frustration   b. frustrate   c. frustrating

3. My parents were bursting with _____ when I graduated from college.
   a. pride   b. proud   c. proudly

4. It's a/(an) _____ you didn't call me. I could have helped you with the children.
   a. shamefully   b. shame   c. ashamed

Unit Tests 107

5. I felt extremely _____ when I did all the work and someone else got all the credit.

   a. resent   b. resentment   c. resentful

1.3 Matching *(6 points)*

Find a word or phrase on the right that has a more specific meaning for the underlined word on the left. Use each choice only once. You will not use all of the choices.

_____ 1. Mr. Michelotti <u>loved</u> his wife.
_____ 2. Mr. Michelotti <u>traveled</u> to his job in Chicago.
_____ 3. Mrs. Michelotti <u>showed</u> the landmarks to her children.
_____ 4. The medical students were <u>tired</u> after working a 36-hour shift.
_____ 5. Hank López <u>walked</u> out of the house in anger.
_____ 6. López <u>took</u> a can of furniture polish and threw it at Mr. Fenner.

a. pointed out
b. stomped
c. stared
d. commuted
e. exhausted
f. was devoted to
g. grabbed

1.4 Writing *(9 points)*

Answer *three* of the questions. Write two to three complete sentences for each answer, using information from the readings in the unit.

1. What do you think are the most important things Mrs. Michelotti does to help her children grow up to be well-balanced, productive adults? Mention at least two things and explain why they are important.
2. What does the anecdote in the furniture store illustrate about Hank López, Mr. Fenner, and Hank's father?
3. What upset José about his sons, and why was this important to him?
4. How has the daughter in "Love, Your Only Mother" been affected by the fact that her mother left the family?

PART TWO
EXPLORING

2.1 Reading

Read the text.

Do Working Moms Make Better Moms?

Kyanna Sutton reports on an interview she had with Joan K. Peters about her book *When Mothers Work: Loving Our Children Without Sacrificing Ourselves.*

1 Kyanna Sutton: In your book, you write that when mothers work, it benefits everyone; mother, father, and child. But some people might argue that women who elect to stay home with their children are actually doing the best thing for their kids. Is being a full-time mom at home an ideal situation for the family?

2 Joan K. Peters: "Mother at home" is the American ideal, but it's peculiarly American. I begin my book with a quote from the great anthropologist, Margaret Mead, about how unique it is for mother to take sole responsibility for children. Jesse Bernard, the "mother" of sociology,[1] offers her view, which is also mine, that a mother-at-home, alone with her children, may be the worst child-rearing arrangement of any culture.

3 KS: How so?

4 JKP: Sociologists cite the cross-cultural studies showing that the more solitary mothering is, the less tender the mothering! This runs exactly counter to our thinking, that only if Mother is always there can she feel the tender maternal bond.

5 I think that if Mother is always there, she is neglecting her identity and growth, which puts her mothering in jeopardy. When women are fulfilled in themselves, they have more to give to children. And women today, raised to fulfill themselves intellectually, financially, and socially rarely feel complete if they give all that up to stay home with small children.

6 KS: In your book you also suggest that moms who work are better models and better moms to their daughters. Why?

7 JKP: Moms who work are better models because they show their children that all people, men and women, get to have work, love, individuality, and family. If they see mothers pursuing "self," it gives them permission to develop their individuality, without feeling guilty or sorry for the mom who gave hers up.

8 Sons with mothers who work develop a respect for women's independence instead of imagining there will always be a woman to "serve" them. The newest long-term study of teens, by the way, noted that divorce or parents working did not affect whether kids turned to drugs, etc. The only relevant factor was parents who were involved in their children's lives. Working doesn't mean you can't be involved in your children's lives.

9 KS: In what ways do women who are moms have to change in order to become more fulfilled individuals and better, happier mothers?

10 JKP: Moms have to change by first sitting down with their partners to create a household they can find rest and joy in. That will often mean making a five-year plan for how the husband (or father of the children) will begin to take greater responsibility for managing the childcare. Perhaps he "takes over" dentist and orthodontist[2] duties, making all the decisions, appointments, etc.

11 Whatever first step he takes means Mother has that much more peace, with which to nurture her children and herself. Often, of course, if Dad cuts back in order to do more childcare, Mother has to assume more financial responsibility, which is often a real challenge for women.

12 KS: You acknowledge that most of the issues you write about with respect to mothers and working are mostly relevant to mainstream white, middle-class mothers. How are the mothering styles of say Latina and African-American women different on the whole from the mothering styles of white middle-class women?

13 JKP: The American ideal of a stay-at-home mom is mostly a white, middle-class phenomenon. African-Americans and Latina women haven't often had the choice to stay home. Because they have to work, they assume that "motherwork" and other work go together. They don't feel the guilt for working; work is part of nurturing your family.

---

[1] **sociology** the study and classification of human societies
[2] **orthodontist** dentist who specializes in correcting the misalignment of teeth

14 African-American sociologists also point out that the African heritage provides a more communal model of raising children than the white American model. Families share in taking care of kids and extended family[3] is usually more closely involved. In this way, African-American mothers can serve as a model for mothering in a less isolated, guilt-driven, exclusive way.

---

[3]**extended family** family that not only includes parents and children, but also grandparents, cousins, aunts, uncles, etc.

2.2 Vocabulary (10 points)

Find the underlined word or expression in the indicated paragraph. Choose the meaning that makes sense in the context.

1. sole (¶2) and solitary (¶4) refer to things that are done
   a. beautifully   b. alone   c. intelligently

2. child-rearing arrangement (¶2) means
   a. way to feed children
   b. way to give medical treatment to children
   c. way to raise children

3. tender (¶4) means
   a. expensive   b. long-term   c. gentle and loving

4. runs exactly counter to (¶4) means
   a. goes against   b. takes time   c. goes fast

5. neglecting (¶5) means
   a. inventing   b. analyzing   c. not paying attention to

6. in jeopardy (¶5) means
   a. in a hurry   b. in danger   c. in good health

7. are fulfilled (¶5) means
   a. are unhappy with life and job
   b. are satisfied with life and job
   c. want to change their lives

8. financially (¶5) and financial (¶11) mean
   a. relating to friendship
   b. relating to beauty
   c. relating to money

9. relevant (¶8) and (¶12) means
   a. important, related   b. old, out-of-date   c. impossible

10. communal (¶14) means
    a. shared by a group   b. uncommon   c. academic

2.3 Comprehension *(10 points)*

Mark the statements T (true) or F (false).

1. **T F** Margaret Mead, Jesse Bernard, and Joan Peters (the author of *When Mothers Work*), all agree with the American belief that it is best for a mother to stay home and raise children.
2. **T F** Studies from different cultures show that mothers give their children the most loving care when they can share the responsibility with other people.
3. **T F** According to Peters, if a mother is always with her children, she is not paying attention to her own needs.
4. **T F** Moms who work are good role models for their daughters but not for their sons.
5. **T F** Children with a working mom get the message that making money is more important to her than her children.
6. **T F** According to this article, if moms work, their children are more likely to be involved with drugs.
7. **T F** The most important factor in raising children is for parents to be involved with their children, not whether they are at home all the time.
8. **T F** Peters recommends that fathers take on some chores to help working mothers.
9. **T F** According to Peters, African-American and Latina women often have to work and therefore feel guiltier about working.
10. **T F** According to Peters, the African-American and Latino cultures provide a model for raising children in ways that relieve pressure on mothers.

Optional Writing Section

If you would like to encourage writing on an exam, use the following question:

According to Peters there are advantages for both mothers and children when mothers work outside the home. What is one benefit for mothers and one for children? Answer in complete sentences.

Benefit for mothers:

_____
_____
_____

Benefit for children:

_____
_____
_____

Name: _____ Date: _____

UNIT 3: STRESS

PART ONE
REVIEWING

1.1 Paragraph Completion (10 points)

Complete the paragraphs with items from the list. Use each item only once.

crisis	depletes	immune	minimize the impact	rate
currently under way	eventually	irritable	prolonged	strategies

There are two kinds of stress: acute and chronic. Mrs. Wynnes, who knew what to do in a(n) (1) _____, handled acute stress well. Chronic stress is perhaps more dangerous because it is (2) _____, and over time it (3) _____ the body's resources for repairing damage.

People under chronic stress are often (4) _____ and need (5) _____ for coping with it, such as taking a 10-minute energy walk or enrolling in an exercise class. If people don't (6) _____ of chronic stress, it may (7) _____ affect their health.

Scientists have known for some time that stress negatively affects the (8) _____ system; current research has discovered that telomere length affects the (9) _____ at which cells age. Research is (10) _____ which will bring us even greater understanding of how stress affects our health.

1.2 Word Families (5 points)

Choose the correct form of the word to complete each sentence.

1. For people who like to be active, _____ can be very stressful.
   a. boring   b. bored   c. boredom

2. The research reported in "Energy Walks" showed that a brisk walk can _____ a person.
   a. energize   b. energetic   c. energetically

3. After doing my exercises, I felt so _____ that I fell asleep easily.
   a. relax   b. relaxing   c. relaxed

4. Aspirin helps to _____ a headache brought on by stress.
   a. relief   b. relieve   c. relieved

5. One way to deal with stress is to imagine a _____ scene.
   a. tranquility   b. tranquil   c. tranquilly

1.3 Matching (6 points)

Match the beginning of the sentence on the left with the correct ending on the right. Use each choice only once. You will not use all of the endings.

_____ 1. Elena had a close
_____ 2. Learn to relax so you don't let stress get
_____ 3. One way to deal with stress is to tune
_____ 4. Research shows that the length of telomeres plays
_____ 5. We need to come up
_____ 6. I feel sorry

a. with some new ideas for relieving stress.
b. with problems.
c. for people who cannot deal with stress well.
d. out of hand.
e. out the comments of people who bother you.
f. a role in how long cells live.
g. call while driving to work.

1.4 Writing (9 points)

Answer *three* of the questions. Write two to three complete sentences for each answer, using information from the readings in the unit.

1. Kopolow gives a number of suggestions for coping with stress. Which *two* do you think are the most effective and why?
2. What was Robert E. Thayer interested in learning about walking? What were his findings?
3. Answer (a) or (b).
   a. What does the article "Stressed to Death" say about how stress affects our cells and therefore our health?
   b. According to the article "Heartfelt Fear," what should doctors ask people who come to the emergency room with the symptoms of a heart attack? Why?
4. How do Mrs. Wynnes and the American naturalist work together to avoid the danger of the cobra and prove that the colonel was wrong about women?

PART TWO
EXPLORING

2.1 Reading

Read the text.

A Kinder, Gentler Exam Week
The new approach to finals <u>stresses</u> low stress

1   In the midst of final exams, a group of students gathered in the natatorium[1] to experience something pretty rare for that time of year: an hour of uninterrupted calm. As they moved gracefully through a series of yoga[2] positions, you could almost see the headaches and hassles of exams melt away, if only temporarily.

---
[1] **natatorium** a building with an indoor swimming pool, among other facilities
[2] **yoga** a general term for a range of body/mind exercises used to access consciousness and encourage physical and mental well-being

2   Traditionally, exam weeks are synonymous with stress. But universities have come around to the notion that finals don't have to be an all-out assault on students' physical and mental well-being. Increasingly, they're offering courses in yoga, meditation,[3] massage,[4] and other stress-busting techniques to help students relieve the pressures of academia.

3   The University of Wisconsin Health Services now employs four massage therapists, offers relaxation classes throughout the semester, and guides a free meditation session on Monday afternoons. They also sponsor classes in yoga and other mind-body exercises, which often fill up during the academic year.

4   "The classes are so popular because they really do help," says Rob Sepich, a stress-management counselor who leads a course on relaxation techniques.

5   Sepich says students often neglect their health because they feel overwhelmed and don't think they have to take a break once in a while. University officials worry that those stresses lead to unhealthy choices, such as cutting back on sleep, eating poorly, or drinking too much. So, in recent years, they've developed new ways to help students learn how to take better care of themselves—from organized discussions and classes to simple reminders about healthy eating and sleeping habits. In his classes, Sepich teaches students techniques they can do on their own time, including muscle relaxation, guided imagery,[5] and even the importance of napping.

6   Shortly before finals each semester, the university sends e-mails to all students with advice on how to maintain a healthy diet and relieve stress during exams, and students are paying attention.

7   "Everyone I know reads those tips," says Melissa Trinley, a student. "People are always looking for suggestions on how to get rid of some of their stress."

8   But that's true for more than just university students. Recent studies have shown that people who experience less stress are generally healthier and recover more quickly from illness or injury than others. Many businesses are beginning to realize that helping workers alleviate stress is a good bottom-line decision. As Sepich notes, it's cheaper to teach people how to cope with stress than it is to deal with potentially serious consequences of too much stress down the line.

---

[3]**meditation** the practice of emptying your mind of thoughts and feelings in order to relax

[4]**massage** the action of pressing and rubbing a person's body to help them relax

[5]**guided imagery** a system that encourages people to use their imagination and thoughts to help them relax (also known as visualization)

2.2 Vocabulary (10 points)

Find the underlined word or expression in the indicated paragraph. Choose the meaning that makes sense in the context.

1. stresses (in the subhead) means

    a. decreases   b. eliminates   c. emphasizes

2. notion (¶2) means

    a. activity   b. idea   c. memory

3. assault (¶2) means

    a. attack   b. help   c. game

4. neglect (¶5) means
   a. think about
   b. don't pay attention to
   c. protect

5. cutting back on (¶5) means
   a. reducing   b. increasing   c. responding to

6. napping (¶5) means
   a. competitive running
   b. sleeping for a short time during the day
   c. working overtime at night

7. get rid of (¶7) means
   a. make use of   b. increase   c. remove

8. alleviate (¶8) means
   a. focus on
   b. get accustomed to
   c. reduce

9. bottom line (¶8) means
   a. financial   b. low-level   c. boring

10. down the line (¶8) means
    a. on the next street   b. in the future   c. in production

2.3 Comprehension (10 points)

A. Mark the statements T (true) or F (false).

1. **T F** Special help to relieve stress is given only during the exam period.
2. **T F** According to the article, stress-management classes are popular because they are free.
3. **T F** One thing Sepich teaches students is that they need breaks from studying.
4. **T F** University officials are concerned that many students don't get enough sleep and don't eat well.
5. **T F** It is reasonable to infer that the university officials are wasting their time trying to help students with stress.
6. **T F** University officials believe it is better to help people reduce stress than to deal with the consequences later.
7. **T F** The article refers only to university students.

B. Answer the questions based on the information in the article.

8. What are two types of help (with stress) that students can get at the University of Wisconsin?
   _____
   _____

9. Why is it good business to help workers reduce stress?
   _____

Name: _____ Date: _____

UNIT 4: CULTURES IN CONTACT

PART ONE
REVIEWING

1.1 Paragraph Completion (10 points)

Complete the paragraphs with items from the list. Use each item only once.

bargaining	biases	get along	innocuous	peasants
bewildering	collide	grasp	invade	standardized

Our culture shapes us to a great extent, and our behavior is more predictable and (1) _____ than we think. What we consider normal in our own culture may seem strange and (2) _____ to people in another culture. For example, rules of touching and personal space can be particularly confusing. What one culture considers a(n) (3) _____ touch may be considered offensive in another. We feel uncomfortable if people get too close and (4) _____ our personal bubble.

Business practices also vary from culture to culture. Therefore, we can expect cultures to (5) _____ when doing business internationally. For example, in some cultures (6) _____ is normal while in others fixed prices are the rule. Mr. Winthrop failed to reach an agreement with the Indian in Mexico because he was not able to (7) _____ the way of thinking of an artist or understand the lifestyle of (8) _____ in a rural area of a developing country.

Cultural differences play an important role when immigrants have to adapt to a new culture. Citizens of the host country also have to make adjustments and put aside their (9) _____ and stereotypes in order to (10) _____ with their new neighbors and co-workers.

1.2 Word Families (5 points)

Choose the correct form of the word to complete each sentence.

1. _____ into a new culture is a slow process, especially for adults.
   a. Assimilate   b. Assimilation   c. Assimilated

2. People are often _____ to speak their second language in public.
   a. hesitant   b. hesitation   c. hesitate

3. When you are in another country, it's a good idea to _____ with the rules of the local culture.
   a. comply   b. compliance   c. compliant

116   World of Reading 3 Teacher's Manual

© 2009 by Pearson Education, Inc. Duplication for classroom use is permitted.

4. The woman reacted _____ when the customs officer would not let her bring fresh fruit into the country.

   a. indignation   b. indignant   c. indignantly

5. Many people feel uncomfortable with a person who has a _____ style.

   a. confront   b. confrontational   c. confrontation

1.3 Matching (6 points)

Match the beginning of the sentence on the left with the correct ending on the right. Use each choice only once. You will not use all of the endings.

_____ 1. Racial
_____ 2. Mary Fischer faced utter
_____ 3. In some cultures, children are taught to avert
_____ 4. The realtor found a prospective
_____ 5. People often have preconceived
_____ 6. He is from a remote

a. notions about other cultures.
b. ends meet.
c. village and has never been to a city.
d. harmony is often difficult to achieve.
e. buyer for the house.
f. despair when she lost her job.
g. their eyes when talking to an adult.

1.4 Writing (9 points)

Answer *three* of the questions. Write two or three complete sentences for each answer, using information from the readings in the unit.

1. According to Kluckhohn, an individual's behavior is formed principally by his/her cultural experience. What are two examples that illustrate this fact? Explain at least one from the reading; the other may be from your own personal experience.
2. What are at least two examples of how rules of touching and personal space affect human behavior?
3. Describe Mary Fischer's "change of heart." Do you think it is typical of citizens of a host country to react to immigrants as she did? Explain.
4. Analyze Mr. Winthrop's character. Why did he fail to make a deal with the Indian?

PART TWO
EXPLORING

2.1 Reading

Read the text

Punctuality: Some Cultures Are Wound Tighter Than Others

Lateness is *de rigueur*[1] one place, rude in another. Don't believe it?
Try arriving early for dinner in Mexico.

1   In Switzerland, the land of watches,[2] trains really do run like clockwork. "If I'm 30 seconds late, the train is gone," said Michelle Kranz, who commutes daily into Lucerne, where she works for the tourist board.

---
[1] ***de riguer*** (French) required
[2] **Switzerland, the land of watches** Switzerland has long been famous for making fine watches and clocks

2   Step across the border, and you're in a different universe. Italy has two rail schedules: the one printed in the brochure[3] and another, flashing updates, on a board in the station. The first may be a fantasy; the second, reality. Next to posted departures, "invariably you see the word '*ritardato*' (delayed)," said Rick Steves, who writes guidebooks and runs a tour company called Europe Through the Back Door in Edmonds, Washington.

3   Your time or my time? When traveling, you're in *their* time. And that can affect almost everything: catching trains and buses, shopping, getting a meal, and making appointments.

4   Knowing a little about the culture can prevent much of the frustration. In some Latin American and southern European nations, hours and minutes seem hardly to matter. In Mexico, guests invited to a 6 P.M. social dinner think nothing of showing up two or three hours later, said Terri Morrison, who is updating a 1995 guide she co-wrote called, "Kiss, Bow or Shake Hands: How to Do Business in More Than Sixty Countries," for release next year. In fact, it's wise to arrive at least an hour late for dinner in Mexico City, Morrison said, to avoid embarrassing an unprepared host.

5   In Switzerland, by contrast, tardiness may be viewed as an insult. In this well-ordered culture, being late is like telling your host: "I had more important things to do than attend your party, so I put it last." No wonder then that Kranz of Swiss tourism said, "If you're invited to dinner at 8, you're ringing the bell at five minutes to 8."

6   Theories abound as to why time doesn't fly at the same speed around the globe. Climate, economics, and culture may play a role. As you get closer to the equator, the pace of life seems to slow, said Andy Case, Latin America analyst for iJET Intelligent Risk Systems, a travel security company based in Annapolis, MD. That might explain the familiar north-versus-south divisions within Europe, the Western Hemisphere, and even within countries. Who cares to race the clock in 100-degree heat?

7   Some economists find truth in the saying "Money is time; time is money." In America, we speak of spending and wasting time as though it *were* money. Under this theory, rich societies move rapidly; poor societies poke along. "Low-income countries have cultures, in general, in which the value of time is relatively low," said Genevieve Giuliano, professor of urban planning and policy at USC. "In places where economic opportunities are limited," she said, "it's easier to give up an hour of work for leisure[4]—or waiting.

8   Russia, where the popularity of punctuality grows as private enterprise expands, lends credence to this theory, said Alex Bobilev, Russian regional manager for iJET. "In the past, you were working for the state," he said. "[Waiting] didn't come out of your pocketbook. Now a lot of people are working for themselves, and the norms are stricter."

9   The most intriguing ideas about how we treat time delve deeply into culture. In his classic 1983 study, "The Dance of Life: The Other Dimension of Time," anthropologist Edward T. Hall used the words "monochronic" and "polychronic" to describe how different societies view time. People in monochronic cultures, such as America and northern Europe, are task-oriented, Hall wrote. They do things in order, one at a time, starting with the most important and ending with the least. Polychronic cultures, found in Mediterranean and many Latin American nations, he said, are "oriented toward people, human relationships and the family, which is the core of their existence." In this world, following a schedule is far less important than catching up with friends and family. Of course, in every society, some people are punctual, some not. Culture just tips the balance.

10   When touring other countries, I've decided, it's best to let time take its course. After all, if you wanted to be immersed in the familiar, you would have never left home. "Learn to breathe, relax," author Morrison advised. "Let the other culture take over a little." And by all means, get to the Swiss train station on time.

---

[3]**brochure** timetable

[4]**leisure** free time

2.2 Vocabulary (10 points)

Find the underlined word or expression in the indicated paragraph. Choose the meaning that makes sense in the context.

1. like clockwork (¶1) means
   a. always on time, punctual
   b. in good mechanical condition
   c. slowly

2. updates (¶2) means
   a. future dates
   b. the most recent information
   c. repeated information

3. tardiness (¶5) means
   a. friendliness   b. lateness   c. punctuality

4. abound (¶6) means
   a. are plentiful   b. are delighted   c. are wrong

5. pace (¶6) means
   a. enjoyment   b. peace   c. speed

6. poke along (¶7) means
   a. move slowly   b. move fast   c. work efficiently

7. lends credence to (¶8) means
   a. gives money to   b. makes believable   c. provides food for

8. intriguing (¶9) means
   a. boring   b. embarrassing   c. interesting

9. delve deeply into (¶9) means
   a. predict correctly   b. produce a lot of   c. examine closely

10. are task-oriented (¶9) means
    a. give importance to things that have to be done
    b. ignore things that have to be done
    c. don't understand things that have to be done

2.3 Comprehension (10 points)

Mark the statements T (true) or F (false).

1. **T F** Trains in both Switzerland and Italy run on time.
2. **T F** In Mexico, if you arrive on time for dinner at someone's house, the host may not be ready.
3. **T F** In Switzerland, if you arrive late for a dinner invitation, the hosts will think you don't consider them important.
4. **T F** One theory about differences in punctuality is that a hot climate makes people hurry.
5. **T F** Another theory is that people are on time in industrialized countries because time is more valuable than in poorer countries.
6. **T F** People in Russia were more punctual under communism when they were working for the government.

7. **T F** According to Edward Hall's theory, in Latin America and southern Europe family and people are more important than time.
8. **T F** Rules of punctuality are followed in a standard way by all members of a culture.
9. **T F** The audience for this article is probably North Americans, who value punctuality.
10. **T F** The author recommends that people should travel to countries where the value placed on time is similar to their own.

UNIT 5 ETHICS

PART ONE
REVIEWING

1.1 Paragraph Completion (10 points)

Complete the paragraphs with items from the list. Use each item only once.

alternative	controversial	empathy	infringe on	victimless crime
confess	copyright	horrified	justified	well-being

Making decisions is not easy because there is almost always more than one (1) _____. When people have differing beliefs and values, an issue can be (2) _____. For example, some people believe that research using animals is (3) _____ because the findings may help humans, but others who have more (4) _____ for animals are (5) _____ by this practice. They urge us to apply the reversibility test and think about the (6) _____ of the animals.

Elaine had to make a decision about helping the battered woman at the toll station. Did she (7) _____ Troy's rights when she gave his money to the woman? Do you think she'll (8) _____ what she did to Troy?

People who decide to violate (9) _____ laws may rationalize their behavior claiming that it's a(n) (10) _____, but if they applied the three tests, they might see things differently.

1.2 Word Families (5 points)

Choose the correct form of the word to complete each sentence.

1. Certainly, the woman that Elaine gave the money to was very _____.
   a. appreciation   b. appreciate   c. appreciative

2. Elaine must be a _____ person.
   a. compassion   b. compassionate   c. compassionately

3. _____ advertising raises numerous ethical questions.
   a. Deception   b. Deceive   c. Deceptive

4. Did you read about the political _____ at the university?
   a. scandal   b. scandalize   c. scandalous

5. Violating copyright laws is a _____ to authors and artists.
   a. threat   b. threaten   c. threatening

1.3 Matching *(6 points)*

Match the beginning of the sentence on the left with the correct ending on the right. Use each choice only once. You will not use all of the endings.

_____ 1. Humane treatment of animals can alleviate
_____ 2. After surgery you will be confined
_____ 3. I don't understand the nature
_____ 4. Chimps are active and social in their natural
_____ 5. The geeks were able to hack
_____ 6. It's important for artists to establish

a. into the professor's computer.
b. a following in order to be successful.
c. economy.
d. unnecessary suffering.
e. to bed for at least a week.
f. habitat.
g. of the problem.

1.4 Writing *(9 points)*

Answer *three* of the questions. Write two to three complete sentences for each answer, using information from the readings in the unit.

1. Suppose you are paid twice for the same job. What do the three ethical tests (consequences, reversibility, and publicity) encourage you to think about before you make your decision about whether to return the extra money or not?
2. Who is negatively affected by the downloading and sharing of copyrighted music? Explain the specific effects on at least two groups of people.
3. What are at least two laboratory conditions that affect chimpanzees mentally or physically? Be sure to describe the effect on chimpanzees.
4. If you were Elaine, would you have given Troy's money to the woman? Why or why not?

PART TWO
EXPLORING

2.1 Reading

Read the text.

Moral Compass

Expert advice on three dilemmas from The Southern Institute for Business and Professional Ethics

Dilemma 1

1 *Complaint:* I'm an advertising executive. For my main client, a fast-food company, food stylists make the burgers look far better than they actually are by using inedible materials such as water sealants.[1] The photos are a glaring misrepresentation. Our ads may have public health consequences, as people eat more and more of these fattening burgers. My work is being praised, but I'm afraid I'm causing heart attacks. What is ethically required?

2 *Response:* You owe your employer and client good service, including ads that sell effectively, as this is what your agency promised when it agreed to accept payment. Yet you're also right to feel obligated to serve the public interest. The American Association of

---
[1]**sealant** a substance that keeps water from going in or out

Advertising Agencies' "Standards of Practice" warn that agencies shouldn't "knowingly create advertising that contains . . . false or misleading statements or <u>exaggerations</u>, visual or verbal." While these standards aren't legally binding—and are often ignored—they provide a starting point for a conversation with colleagues, which is where you should begin your effort to resolve the dilemma. What guidance does your agency offer? Perhaps it has its own code of ethics. If not, it should.

Dilemma 2

3   *Complaint:* I'm a low-level employee at a waste-treatment facility near the Mexican border that is exceeding the legal limit for dumping a potentially harmful toxin.[2] When I voice concern to my superiors, I'm told to keep quiet. The plant fuels the small town's economy. If I report it, the plant will likely move across the border, where restrictions are less <u>stringent</u>. The environmental damage will be the same either way. What should I do?

4   *Response:* Let's begin by checking your assumptions. A self-described "low-level employee" may lack enough knowledge to conclude that reporting the problem will result in the plant's moving to Mexico. Likewise, if the company is bending the more-stringent U.S. environmental laws, it is likely to do more damage in a country where the regulatory structure is less developed and poorly enforced. Assuming the company is larger than one plant, senior management may not share the attitude of the superiors who told you to keep quiet. <u>Environmental compliance</u> is a <u>high priority</u> for most U.S. companies, because it has to be. There are many cases where employee reports of this type have led to improvements for all concerned.

Dilemma 3

5   *Complaint:* My boss makes vulgar, inappropriate comments to me, but I'm used to it and value my job. Still, I worry that by not reporting him I'm enabling the future <u>harassment</u> of my colleagues. What are my moral obligations?

6   *Response:* Your fear for your job is understandable, and it can be very uncomfortable to make an accusation of this kind, especially since your manager is likely to deny it. You may not be legally required to report him, but you do have a moral obligation to do so, for your own <u>sake</u>, the sake of other employees, and even for the sake of the company itself. You may not choose to <u>sue</u> the company, but allowing a <u>predator</u> to continue this sort of behavior will lead to a costly legal claim sooner or later.

---

[2]**dumping a potentially harmful toxin** disposing of a possibly dangerous or poisonous substance

2.2 Vocabulary *(10 points)*

Find the underlined word or expression in the indicated paragraph. Choose the meaning that makes sense in the context.

1. <u>dilemmas</u> (in the subtitle) means
   a. section headings
   b. situations requiring a difficult choice
   c. solutions to serious problems

2. <u>a glaring misrepresentation</u> (¶1) means
   a. bright and attractive   b. very effective   c. completely dishonest

3. <u>exaggerations</u> (¶2) means
   a. statements that are very critical
   b. statements that make something seem better than it really is
   c. very colorful pictures

4. <u>stringent</u> (¶3) means
   a. delightful   b. long   c. strict

5. <u>environmental compliance</u> (¶4) means
   a. following environmental regulations
   b. refusing to follow environmental regulations
   c. writing environmental regulations

6. <u>high priority</u> (¶4) means
   a. very important   b. difficult to do   c. easy to do

7. <u>harassment</u> (¶5) means
   a. education
   b. offensive treatment
   c. psychological evaluation

8. <u>sake</u> (¶6) means
   a. benefit   b. style   c. surprise

9. <u>sue</u> (¶6) means
   a. ask for
   b. bring a legal case against
   c. question the honesty of

10. <u>predator</u> (¶6) means
    a. one person pursuing another
    b. marathon runner
    c. senior citizen

2.3 Comprehension (10 points)

Mark the statements *T* (true) or *F* (false).

Dilemma 1

1. **T F** We can infer that hamburgers in ads often look better than they do in real life.
2. **T F** Ad agencies have an obligation to their clients but not to the public.
3. **T F** We can infer that ad agencies are supposed to have guidelines to help make ethical decisions.

Dilemma 2

4. **T F** When environmental laws are too strict, companies may leave the country.
5. **T F** The employee with the problem is the manager of the plant.
6. **T F** The advice is to report the problem to the highest management.
7. **T F** Reporting such problems rarely brings results.

Dilemma 3

8. **T F** The person filing the complaint is primarily concerned about other employees who might have a similar problem in the future.
9. **T F** The advice is to bring a lawsuit against the company.
10. **T F** The person responding believes that someone will sue the company eventually if the problem is not reported.

124 *World of Reading 3 Teacher's Manual*

UNIT 6: THE ENVIRONMENT

PART ONE: REVIEWING

1.1 Paragraph Completion (10 points)

Complete the paragraphs with items from the list. Use each item only once.

accelerating	cut down on	deplete	shift	unsustainable
biodegradable	demand	replenish	stabilize	wind up

In this unit you read about some of the environmental problems we are facing. Underlying them is the fact that the population of the world is increasing at a(n) (1) _____ rate, and there are not enough resources to support us all as we would like to live.

Wealthier countries in particular have a(n) (2) _____ lifestyle. They consume far too much energy from non-renewable sources; they use far too many disposable items that (3) _____ in landfills instead of being reused or recycled. If this waste is not (4) _____, it stays in the landfill forever.

Rich and poor nations alike (5) _____ forests faster than nature can (6) _____ them. They cut down trees for firewood, to build houses, or to use the land to meet the increasing (7) _____ for meat. Environmental pessimists think it is already too late to save our planet, but optimists think there is still time to (8) _____ the population, (9) _____ to renewable sources of energy, (10) _____ the amount of meat we eat, and find other ways to save our planet.

1.2 Word Families (5 points)

Choose the correct form of the word to complete each sentence.

1. There are special requirements for the _____ of chemical waste in the United States.
   a. disposal   b. dispose   c. disposable

2. We see a great deal of _____ in the ways that countries are trying to reduce their carbon footprint.
   a. diverse   b. diversified   c. diversity

3. Our school environmental program _____ accepted a donation to help us plant trees.
   a. gratitude   b. gratefully   c. grateful

4. Our environmental organization is planning a campaign to call people's attention to the _____ of lakes and rivers in our state.
   a. polluted   b. pollution   c. pollute
5. We must learn to spend our natural capital _____.
   a. wisdom   b. wise   c. wisely

1.3 Matching (6 points)

Match the beginning of the sentence on the left with the correct ending on the right. Use each choice only once. You will not use all of the endings.

_____ 1. There's no time
_____ 2. Some countries use more than their fair
_____ 3. The U.S. definitely doesn't lead the
_____ 4. Species become
_____ 5. Our neighbors built a solar house from
_____ 6. Everyone must make an effort to go

a. green.
b. way in mass transportation.
c. to shame.
d. share of natural resources.
e. to spare if we want to save our planet.
f. scratch.
g. extinct as a result of natural and human causes.

1.4 Writing (9 points)

Answer *three* of the questions. Write two to three complete sentences for each answer, using information from the readings in the unit.

1. What does it mean to live sustainably? What is one way that humans are not living sustainably and what are the consequences? Consider, for example, forests, energy, air, soil, and water.
2. Which idea for making life in a city more sustainable did you find most interesting? How will this idea help people live better with less negative impact on the environment?
3. Answer (a) or (b).
   a. How will eating less meat positively affect the environment?
   b. Why is most of the plastic we use and the way we handle it bad for the environment?
4. The environmental science textbook describes three worldviews: planetary management, stewardship, and environmental wisdom. Define each briefly. Which is your view and why do you believe it is the best view to have?

PART TWO
EXPLORING

2.1 Reading

Read the text.

Environmental Tipping Points[1]:
A New Slant on Strategic Environmentalism

1 Apo Island, thirty minutes from the coast of Negros, in the Philippines, was a paradise[2] almost lost. Twenty-five years ago, like countless communities around the world, islanders found their livelihood headed for collapse. Fishing had always been the foundation of the village economy, and the fish were disappearing.

2 What saved their fishery and their way of life was that they found a positive environmental tipping point.

3 Day by day, we're flooded with news of environmental devastation. We read that natural systems, from rainforests to ocean currents, are nearing "tipping points" of irreversible change. But around the globe, a positive kind of environmental tipping point is quietly emerging, one that tips towards sustainability instead of away from it.

4 Like many other fishing villages in the Philippines, where fish stocks have dropped as much as 95 percent in the past 50 years, Apo had been in a slow decline. Population growth had triggered heavier fishing. New methods of fishing were more effective but more destructive than traditional ones. Over time, fishermen were traveling farther and working harder to catch fish that became ever scarcer, as they exhausted one fishing ground after another.

5 The rescue of Apo Island began with Angel Alcala, a marine biologist from Siliman University in nearby Dumaguete City. Based on his prior experience at another island, he proposed a small change. Banning fishing on around 10 percent of the island could create a nursery[3] from which to repopulate adjacent fishing grounds. "We already had proof that no-take marine reserves[4] increased fishermen's catch, enhanced fisheries, and maintained coral reefs,[5]" says Alcala. "Marine reserves allow fish to grow larger before they're caught. They allow fish to mature and reproduce."

6 In 1982, 14 families began guarding the coral-covered fishing grounds off a 450-meter strip of beach. After three years, the resulting explosion of aquatic[6] life convinced other islanders to make the sanctuary[7] official. At the same time, they prohibited destructive fishing methods throughout Apo's waters. They set up a volunteer marine guard to enforce the rules and keep out fishermen who weren't from the island. Within 10 years, fish stocks had rebounded so much that fishermen could pull in a day's catch within 500 meters from shore.

---

[1]**tipping point** the point at which negative change can no longer be stopped or reversed

[2]**paradise** ideal, extremely beautiful place

[3]**nursery** place to raise fish (in this example)

[4]**reserve** protected place

[5]**coral reef** corals are marine organisms that live in colonies (groups) in warm water and form long, hard underwater structures (reefs), which are good habitats for fish

[6]**aquatic** related to water

[7]**sanctuary** protected place

7   The lever of a marine reserve had tipped Apo's vicious cycle of destruction into virtuous cycles of reconstruction, growing stronger and stronger over time:

- Less-intensive fishing produced more fish, which meant even less need for <u>aggressive</u> methods. Fishermen worked fewer hours and could earn extra money at other jobs.
- Habitat protection led to healthier reefs, which reeled in tourists. Extra income for infrastructure and education strengthened islanders' <u>resolve</u> to safeguard the habitat.
- Islanders controlled tourism to protect <u>fragile</u> reefs and adopted family planning, so the next generation won't overrun the fishery.
- Following Apo's lead, more than 400 other Philippine villages have started marine sanctuaries.

8   As positive changes <u>gain momentum</u>, environmental tips, like Apo's tip, become harder to reverse; nature and natural social processes do most of the work of rebuilding. Success <u>breeds</u> success, <u>rejuvenating</u> more and more of an eco-social system.

2.2 Vocabulary *(10 points)*

Find the underlined word or expression in the indicated paragraph. Choose the meaning that makes sense in the context.

1. devastation (¶3) means
   a. renewal   b. destruction   c. education

2. irreversible (¶3) means
   a. cannot be turned around
   b. cannot be elected
   c. cannot be studied

3. exhausted (¶4) means
   a. used up   b. improved   c. tired

4. rebounded (¶6) means
   a. stopped growing
   b. gotten much smaller
   c. come back to good condition

5. aggressive (¶7) means
   a. impolite
   b. strong
   c. talkative

6. resolve (¶7) means
   a. contribution   b. education   c. determination

7. fragile (¶7) means
   a. healthy   b. not strong, weak   c. old-fashioned

8. gain momentum (¶8) means
   a. increase speed   b. earn money   c. waste time

9. breeds (¶8)
   a. leads to   b. stops   c. cleans

10. <u>rejuvenating</u> (¶8) means
    a. destroying again
    b. making something strong again
    c. talk about again

2.3 Comprehension *(10 points)*

Mark the statements *T* (true) or *F* (false).

1. **T F** Fishing declined around Apo Island because of destructive fishing methods and the need to feed a growing population.
2. **T F** Angel Alcala convinced the islanders to turn half the waters around the island into a protected place with no fishing.
3. **T F** Benefits of a marine nursery or reserve are that fish have a chance to grow bigger and to reproduce before they are caught.
4. **T F** The Apo islanders welcomed fishermen from other islands.
5. **T F** In about 10 years fishermen could earn their living near the island.
6. **T F** Once the fishing stocks were back in good condition, fishermen could take a second job and earn more money.
7. **T F** Among the benefits of better fishing were increased tourism, better infrastructure (such as roads), and better schools.
8. **T F** Apo Islanders let any number of tourists come to their coral reefs.
9. **T F** The success story of Apo Island is unique in the Philippine Islands.
10. **T F** It is reasonable to infer that this environmental tipping point cost millions of dollars.

Unit Tests
Answer Key

Note that answers for the Writing sections of the tests are only suggestions to give teachers an idea of what to look for in students' answers. It is up to teachers to determine how they evaluate use of vocabulary, writing style, and grammatical accuracy. Furthermore, students will undoubtedly come up with other good answers, perhaps based on class discussion, which certainly should be accepted.

UNIT 1 FRIENDSHIP

PART ONE

1.1 Paragraph Completion

1. enrich
2. intersect
3. peers
4. exposure
5. promotes
6. keeping up with
7. Furthermore
8. ongoing
9. intensity
10. critical

1.2 Word Families

1. b
2. b
3. a
4. b
5. c

1.3 Matching

1. d
2. g
3. e
4. f
5. a
6. c

1.4 Writing

1. Students should discuss two of the four categories. Note that you should accept similar examples (of favors, activities) from a student's own experience.
   Convenience: Convenience friends do each other favors such as giving rides to each other's kids, taking care of each other's pets when one goes on vacation, and lending each other things. Convenience friends are often neighbors or co-workers; they are not usually close friends.
   Special Interest: Special interest friends share an activity or interest. For example, they may play a sport together, take a class together, or they may be activists for the same cause. They do things together but are not usually very close friends.
   Cross-Generational: Cross-generational friendships involve people of different ages. The younger person can get good advice from the older, more experienced one. In addition, young people are more likely to listen to an adult who is not their parent. The older person benefits from contact with a younger generation. There are many benefits, among them understanding new ways of doing things.
   Close: Close friends are always there for each other. They confide in each other, they help each other when either one has a problem, and they should be honest with each other. Close friends make our lives easier and more fun. Sometimes they are more important to us than family. (Reference could be made to the quotes on the Unit Opener page.)

2. Reference should be made to ideas in "Online Friendships" and should include some detail.

3. With technology, **proximity** is less important than it used to be; people make friends and maintain friendships online across great distances. The **exposure** people have to each other is not always face-to-face, but it is still necessary to have ongoing contact. **Similarity** is also still important, but we establish what we have in common in different ways. Beware that it may be easier to falsify similarity online than it is in the real world. **Physical attractiveness** probably still plays a role, but it too is easier to falsify online than in person.

4. Making friends in school is important for all children. In the case of Jim Davy, however, it was especially important because he was an only child; his mother had died, and his father was a rather distant parent.

Unit Tests Answer Key 131

PART TWO

2.2 Vocabulary

1. b
2. a
3. a
4. c
5. c
6. a
7. c
8. b
9. a
10. c

2.3 Comprehension

1. F (¶1)
2. T (¶1)
3. T (¶3–5; note also general statement at end of ¶2)
4. F (¶3)
5. F (¶6)
6. T (¶7)
7. T (¶7–8)
8. F (¶8)
9. F (¶9)
10. T (¶10–11)

UNIT 2: PARENTS AND CHILDREN

PART ONE

1.1 Paragraph Completion

1. nurture
2. potential
3. accomplish
4. hectic
5. wonder
6. urge
7. puzzled
8. pursue
9. convince
10. thrive

1.2 Word Families

1. c
2. a
3. a
4. b
5. c

1.3 Matching

1. f
2. d
3. a
4. e
5. b
6. g

1.4 Writing

1. Students should mention at least two of the following: Mrs. Michelotti bolsters her children's self-confidence. There are many examples of this: she helps them with schoolwork; she leads field trips; she encourages them to pursue a profession; she sets an example of generosity by helping others; she develops their sense of family and teaches them to honor and support each other; she doesn't want things for herself. Be sure students explain why they consider these things important.

2. The incident in the furniture store illustrates how sensitive Hank was about his father's illiteracy and inability to sign his name. It shows how easily Hank got angry. The incident also illustrates that Mr. Fenner was a nasty person and that Mr. López was very humble.

3. José was upset when his sons decided to leave California to strike out on their own, probably because he had a strong sense of family and wanted to keep the family together. He apparently hoped that his sons would continue to work with him. What he wanted was based on his own culture, while his sons were learning American values.

4. The daughter in this story is confused and has conflicting feelings. She feels abandoned by her mother, yet she is afraid that her mother will return. She spends time going through the postcards and trying to figure out what they mean, where they come from, how her mother knows where she is, what really happened to her mother, etc. She has nightmares that her mother has returned.

World of Reading 3 Teacher's Manual

PART TWO

2.2 Vocabulary

1. b
2. c
3. c
4. a
5. c
6. b
7. b
8. c
9. a
10. a

2.3 Comprehension

1. F (¶1)
2. T (¶4)
3. T (¶5)
4. F (¶7–8)
5. F (no mention)
6. F (¶8)
7. T (¶8)
8. T (¶10)
9. F (¶13)
10. T (¶14)

Optional Writing Section

Benefit for mothers: Students should mention the idea that when mothers work outside the home, they benefit by being able to fulfill themselves intellectually, financially, and socially, and therefore have more to give to their children.

Benefit for children: Students should mention the idea that when mothers work outside the home, children see that all people get to have work, love, individuality, and family.

UNIT 3: STRESS

PART ONE

1.1 Paragraph Completion

1. crisis
2. prolonged
3. depletes
4. irritable
5. strategies
6. minimize the impact
7. eventually
8. immune
9. rate
10. currently under way

1.2 Word Families

1. c
2. a
3. c
4. b
5. b

1.3 Matching

1. g
2. d
3. e
4. f
5. a
6. c

1.4 Writing

1. Answers should include specific reference to at least two of the following: physical activity, talking to others, knowing your limits, taking care of your own health, having fun, being a participant, being organized and prioritizing tasks, being flexible, crying if necessary, imagining a tranquil scene (relaxation technique), and being careful about medication. Be sure students give reasons.
2. Thayer was interested in the effect of walking on mood. He found that a 10-minute brisk walk made people feel more energized and alert than a sugar snack. These walks increased energy for a substantial time, reduced tension, made problems seem less serious, and even helped people quit smoking. The effect lasted an hour or longer and did not depend on surroundings.
3a. Chronic stress apparently wears down and shortens telomeres, which makes cells age faster. They stop dividing and die, affecting the health of the body's organs.
3b. Emergency room doctors should ask patients with heart attack symptoms if they have recently had a stressful or traumatic experience. The acute stress of a traumatic experience can cause some symptoms of

heart attacks even if arteries are not clogged. Such events release catecholamine hormones into the blood causing heart attack-like symptoms, which disappear over time.

4. Mrs. Wynnes calmly asks a servant to place a bowl of milk on the veranda to get the snake to leave the dining room. The American naturalist is aware of what she is doing and gets everyone to stay quiet for five minutes by challenging them to a bet. Mrs. Wynnes's calm behavior proves that the Colonel was wrong when he said that women can't handle even small crises such as seeing a mouse.

2.3 Comprehension

A.
1. F (¶3) 5. F (¶7)
2. F (¶4) 6. T (¶8)
3. T (¶5) 7. F (¶8)
4. T (¶5)

B.
8. Two of the following: classes in techniques that reduce stress (yoga, muscle relaxation, guided imagery, meditation, massage), organized discussions, e-mail reminders about healthy eating, and getting enough sleep
9. It's a form of preventive medicine. We can infer that stress reduction will result in less lost work time from stress-induced illnesses, saving businesses money.

PART TWO

2.2 Vocabulary

1. c   5. a   9. a
2. b   6. b   10. b
3. a   7. c
4. b   8. c

UNIT 4: CULTURES IN CONTACT

PART ONE

1.1 Paragraph Completion

1. standardized
2. bewildering
3. innocuous
4. invade
5. collide
6. bargaining
7. grasp
8. peasants
9. biases
10. get along

1.2 Word Families

1. b   3. a   5. b
2. a   4. c

1.3 Matching

1. d   3. g   5. a
2. f   4. e   6. c

1.4 Writing

1. One example that illustrates how culture has a stronger influence on behavior than we think is the case of the son of American parents who was raised by Chinese people in China. His behavior was completely Chinese, and he felt out of place in the U.S. What we are willing to eat is also shaped by our culture. This is illustrated by the people who got sick when they found out they were eating rattlesnake meat even though it tasted good before they knew what it was.
2. In Japan, for example, people do not feel comfortable with physical contact. In crowded public places touching from the elbow up is acceptable as long as there is

no eye contact (also true among North Americans). According to Axtell, it's difficult for a Japanese man to tolerate a friendly slap on the back from an American. Another example is Arab men who might hold hands as a sign of friendship and respect, whereas many other cultures find this most unusual. Other examples students might mention: Koreans who put change on the counter rather than in a customer's hand. In terms of personal space: participants in the conversational tango who have different cultural rules about personal space.

3. Mary Fischer, a North American, moved into an interethnic neighborhood where there were many things that bothered her, such as roosters and loud music. Like many natives of a host country, she felt her neighbors should assimilate to the norms of her country. However, when she suffered some personal hardships, she became more willing to get to know her neighbors and ended up understanding and liking them.

4. Mr. Winthrop was a narrow-minded, ethnocentric North-American businessman. Because he was so close-minded, he couldn't understand what the Indian was telling him—that it was impossible to mass-produce the handmade baskets that Mr. Winthrop wanted. Mr. Winthrop's mind was focused only on the money he thought he could make.

PART TWO

2.2 Vocabulary

1. a
2. b
3. b
4. a
5. c
6. a
7. b
8. c
9. c
10. a

2.3 Comprehension

1. F (¶1–2)
2. T (¶4)
3. T (¶5)
4. F (¶6)
5. T (¶7)
6. F (¶8)
7. T (¶9)
8. F (¶9)
9. T (source is a U.S. newspaper; The writer is addressing people who think punctuality is the norm.)
10. F (¶10)

UNIT 5 ETHICS

PART ONE

1.1 Paragraph Completion

1. alternative
2. controversial
3. justified
4. empathy
5. horrified
6. well-being
7. infringe on
8. confess
9. copyright
10. victimless crime

1.2 Word Families

1. c
2. b
3. c
4. a
5. a

1.3 Matching

1. d
2. e
3. g
4. f
5. a
6. b

1.4 Writing

1. If I keep the extra money, I'll be better off, so the <u>consequences</u> for me could be good. If I apply the <u>reversibility</u> test, I will realize that the person who paid me is losing money, and I would not like that to happen to me. If all my co-workers found out that I kept the money (<u>publicity</u> test), I might lose their trust, which I would not like.

2. Students should mention two of the following: the performers, the composers and accompanying musicians, music

companies, people who work in music stores, warehouses, or any facility that is part of the chain that sells music to the public. Everyone loses money when there are fewer sales. Jobs in stores and other aspects of selling music will be lost. Music companies will not support new musicians if they can't make a profit, and in the end less music will be produced, so even the consumer loses.

3. Students can mention such things as: size of cages, lack of stimulating playthings, lack of comfort, and lack of companionship—whether human or chimp. Lack of companionship will cause depression while boredom and confinement often lead to insanity. The animals' immune systems are likely to be affected, and the animals will get sick. These poor health conditions, both mental and physical, make the chimps bad subjects for research and jeopardize the value of the research.

4. Look for specific reasons and application of the three tests.

PART TWO

2.2 Vocabulary

1. b   5. a   9. b
2. c   6. a   10. a
3. b   7. b
4. c   8. a

2.3 Comprehension

1. T (¶1)   6. T (¶4)
2. F (¶2)   7. F (¶4)
3. T (¶2)   8. T (¶5)
4. T (¶3)   9. F (¶6)
5. F (¶3)   10. T (¶6)

UNIT 6 THE ENVIRONMENT

PART ONE

1.1 Paragraph Completion

1. accelerating
2. unsustainable
3. wind up
4. biodegradable
5. deplete
6. replenish
7. demand
8. stabilize
9. shift
10. cut down on

1.2 Word Families

1. a   3. b   5. c
2. c   4. b

1.3 Matching

1. e   3. b   5. f
2. d   4. g   6. a

1.4 Writing

1. To live sustainably is to live within our means and not use more resources than we have or consume them faster than they can be replenished. When we destroy forests without replanting them and allow topsoil to erode, we are living unsustainably because future generations will not be able to grow enough food. When we pollute the oceans, we kill the supply of fish for food or make them unsafe to eat. If we use up non-renewable sources of energy (petroleum, natural gas, and coal) before we switch to renewable sources, our economies will fail. In addition, the burning of fossil fuels pollutes the air we breathe and accelerates global warming.

2. Students should discuss one of the following:

ACTIONS	BENEFITS
increasing mass transportation, green buildings, and green space (Portland, U.S.A.)	uses less energy, provides more trees and natural space to enjoy
making the city less car friendly: bike ways, pedestrian zones, light rail systems, and plans to ban all cars during rush hour (Bogatá, Columbia and Groningen, Holland)	reduces carbon emissions and improves the quality of the air we breathe
planting trees, installing drains, and making streets porous to capture rainwater, which usually runs off (Los Angeles, U.S.A.)	reuses fresh water in an area where it is often scarce
developing good farmers' markets (Pittsburgh, U.S.A.)	makes good local food available and supports local farmers and the local economy
creating wildlife corridors (Rio de Janiero, Brazil)	promotes and increases natural habitats and biodiversity
building large-scale, sustainable housing projects (Johannesburg, South Africa and Peabody, England)	uses less energy
building new cities using green architecture, putting farms on roofs (China)	green architecture uses less energy, rooftop gardens substitute for some of the agricultural land taken to build houses and provide food

3a. The meat industry contributes more greenhouse-gas emissions than cars, trucks, planes, and ships. If people eat less meat, meat production will be reduced and so will greenhouse gas emissions. Furthermore, a great deal of land and fresh water are used to grow grain to feed animals raised for meat, and factory farms pollute our water systems.

3b. Most of the plastic we use is not biodegradable. It ends up in landfills or the oceans where it lasts forever and endangers marine life. Even plastic that is recyclable is not usually recycled.

4. People who have a planetary management worldview believe that nature exists for the benefit of humans. People who have a stewardship worldview also believe that nature exists for human benefit but that we must manage it responsibly. People who have an environmental wisdom worldview believe that nature exists for the benefit of all species and encourage humans to live sustainably. (Additional comments will vary.)

PART TWO

2.2 Vocabulary

1. b
2. a
3. a
4. c
5. b
6. c
7. b
8. a
9. a
10. b

2.3 Comprehension

1. T (¶4)
2. F (¶5)
3. T (¶5–6)
4. F (¶6)
5. T (¶6)
6. T (¶7, 1st bullet)
7. T (¶7, 2nd bullet)
8. F (¶7, 3rd bullet)
9. F (¶7, 4th bullet)
10. F (¶5–6, no mention of cost)